Power Currency

Power Currency

How to Grow, Enhance, and Stop Squandering Your Personal Power!

DR. FRED LEHR

RAND-SMITH PUBLISHING
ASHLAND, VA USA

POWER CURRENCY: How to Grow, Enhance, and Stop Squandering Your Personal Power!

Copyright 2020 Fred Lehr
All rights reserved

Print ISBN: 978-1-950544-24-0 (paperback)
Digital ISBN: 978-1-950544-25-7

Registered with the Library of Congress

Myers-Briggs Type Indicator®, Myers-Briggs®, and MBTI® are trademarks or registered trademarks of the Myers-Briggs Type Indicator Trust in the United States and other countries.

Rand-Smith Publishing
www.Rand-Smith.com

Ashland, VA

Contents

Dedication

I want to dedicate this book to my family. It was their idea to write this kind of book for a wide audience.

To my wife, who is my heart and soul. Without her I am incomplete.

To my son, who challenges all my assumptions.

To my daughter, who inspires me in so many ways.

Introduction

Power! Not just power, but personal power! Personal power is gained through intentionally living by a set of standards and skills that enhance your ability to get what you want.

In our personal power – family power – relationship power – organizational power (especially in non-profit organizations) – and even corporate power – most of us are so poor at the way we use that power that we squander its impact and effectiveness all the time. The amount of power and influence we waste is enormous. We are fully capable of having and exercising much more power than we can usually imagine.

This book presents a comprehensive analysis of empowerment and the concepts behind it. We will explore the meaning of power, where we get our empowerment and how we can use it more effectively.

Power Currency! examines the value of previously identified wisdom not typically applied to the discussion of empowerment and gives it new application. You may well find yourself thinking, "Oh, I know about that. But I never thought of it this way!"

This book is a compilation of a lifetime of learning. I am taking things familiar to many and casting them in a new light focused on the utilization of personal power. So, the familiar will be set in a new way for additional insights and learning.

The sources for this effort are varied. One primary source no longer exists – the Mid-Atlantic Association for Training and Consulting. I am a student of that group and have benefited from its teachings over the decades. They did excellent work.

Other familiar sources like the Myers-Briggs Type Indicator® ([MBTI®] from the Consulting Psychologists Press, Palo Alto, Calif.) will be presented with the lens of empowerment gaining new insights. These recognizable sources have merit on their own but also serve anew in our greater understanding of empowerment. For example, using the MBTI – "Why do I get along better with some folks than with others, and how can I be more influential with those whom I don't easily resonate?"

The field of codependence will be viewed from the lens of empowerment. "Why do I allow others to treat me the way I do" – or – "Why do I feel the need to control others?"

What is the currency of power, and what do we mean by "long-term self-interest?" What does "systems theory" have to say about empowerment? And how do the actions of John Wayne and Mahatma K. Gandhi come into play?

By weaving together new insights with familiar sources, this comprehensive analysis will glean a wider range of wisdom and application from new and old. Just because we are familiar with a source does not mean we have "mined" all we can get from it. There is more to be gained when approached from the perspective of empowerment.

To be clear, I mean to dive deep into the holistic essence of power – body, mind and spirit – in ways new and fresh. Explore anew the gems I have collected over the seventy-plus years of my life and take hold of their precious value anew.

To understand these concepts more easily, I have used financial symbolism because we all understand the power and importance of money and how it can affect our power. There is a Personal Power Portfolio Checkup at the beginning of this book to help assess your current understanding of personal power. Then, each chapter has a section called "Building Your Power Portfolio" that contains carefully curated questions designed to help you think a little differently about your personal power

Once you have read through the chapters and "Building Your Power Portfolio" questions, there is another Personal Power Portfolio Checkup at the end of the book. When you answer those questions, you should see a noticeable improvement in your responses after applying the personal power concepts.

So, journey with me as we venture through new and old and knit them together in this comprehensive analysis designed to enhance your understanding of personal power, learn how to use it more productively and stop giving so much of it away.

Initial Personal Power Portfolio Checkup

For each item, note the response that most accurately defines your *actions most of the time.*

1. Have you lost sleep because of the behavior (i.e. comments, etc.) of someone else?

   Never   Seldom   Sometimes   Often

2. Have you extracted one or more promises from a friend or family member regarding *their behavior* toward you or others which that person did not keep?

   Never   Seldom   Sometimes   Often

3. Do many or most of your thoughts revolve around issues with your family/friends/colleagues around their behaviors?

   Never   Seldom   Sometimes   Often

4. Do you make decisions and not follow through with them; especially if you are worried about how that decision might impact another?

   Never   Seldom   Sometimes   Often

5. Has your attitude changed/fluctuated toward one or more members of your family, friends, colleagues? (For example: alternating between love and anger or contempt or indifference)

Never   Seldom   Sometimes   Often

6. Do you think everything would be okay if only a troublesome member of your family, a friend, a colleague would stop or control his/her troublesome behavior?

Never   Seldom   Sometimes   Often

7. Have your moods changed drastically as a result of a member of your family, a friend, a colleague's mood or behavior?

Never   Seldom   Sometimes   Often

8. Do you feel guilty and/or responsible for the mood or behavior of a family member, friend, or colleague?

Never   Seldom   Sometimes   Often

9. Do you try to conceal or deny problems, make excuses, or protect a member of your family, a friend, a colleague?

Never   Seldom   Sometimes   Often

10. Have you withdrawn from outside activities and/or social contacts because of worry over the behavior of a family member, a friend, a colleague?

Never   Seldom   Sometimes   Often

11. Have you withdrawn from outside activities and/or friends because you were too busy or too tired?

Never   Seldom   Sometimes   Often

12. Have you taken over responsibilities or duties that were formerly done by a member of your family, a friend, a colleague

should have done?

Never   Seldom   Sometimes   Often

13. Do you feel hopeless and defeated, that nothing you can do will improve the situation?

Never   Seldom   Sometimes   Often

14. Do you feel you give more than you receive in relationships?

Never   Seldom   Sometimes   Often

15. Is it difficult for you to feel good about yourself when others are angry or critical of you?

Never   Seldom   Sometimes   Often

16. Do you have difficulty expressing your feelings, especially anger, because of fear about how others will react?

Never   Seldom   Sometimes   Often

17. Do you say "yes" when you would like to say "no," do things for others that you resent, or feel guilty when you say "no" to others?

Never   Seldom   Sometimes   Often

18. Do you try to appear cheerful when you're hurting inside?

Never   Seldom   Sometimes   Often

19. Have you violated the privacy of others in order to check up on them? (For example: reading their mail, checking their e-mail or voice mail, etc.)

Never   Seldom   Sometimes   Often

20. Have you violated your own values in order to avoid conflict or feel accepted or connected with others?

Never   Seldom   Sometimes   Often

21. Have you done many things for others that they could do for themselves because you enjoy feeling needed?

Never   Seldom   Sometimes   Often

22. Have you done many things for others that they could do for themselves because you think you can do it better than they would, or you don't want to inconvenience them?

Never   Seldom   Sometimes   Often

23. Do you not tell others about your problems because you don't trust they will really care or understand, and you don't like to bother them?

Never   Seldom   Sometimes   Often

24. Do you pride yourself in your ability to go without and to endure pain and hardship?

Never   Seldom   Sometimes   Often

25. Have you neglected your own responsibilities and your performance has suffered because of your worry about others?

Never   Seldom   Sometimes   Often

26. Have you been engaging in some behaviors (for example: eating, working, drinking, sex, gambling, spending, etc.) more

than you feel comfortable with?

Never   Seldom   Sometimes   Often

27. Do you feel somewhat righteous or superior to others?

Never   Seldom   Sometimes   Often

28. Are you unhappy when a member of your family, a friend, a colleague is unhappy or is behaving inappropriately?

Never   Seldom   Sometimes   Often

29. Has your relationship with another been affected by feelings of anger, fear, contempt, disappointment, or distrust?

Never   Seldom   Sometimes   Often

30. Do you think that if the troublesome other really liked you they would stop their problematic behavior?

Never   Seldom   Sometimes   Often

31. Do you feel if you could just try harder to be more pleasant, patient, fun, interesting, exciting, or kind the troublesome other would stop their problematic behavior?

Never   Seldom   Sometimes   Often

32. Are you afraid that other people blame you for the troublesome behavior of another?

Never   Seldom   Sometimes   Often

33. Have you been physically or verbally abusive to a troublesome other when angry or upset about that person's behavior?

Never   Seldom   Sometimes   Often

34. Do you feel more like a parent to a friend or colleague?

Never   Seldom   Sometimes   Often

35. Do you feel forced to exert tight control over another with less and less success, while financial problems increase?

Never   Seldom   Sometimes   Often

36. Have you been angry or impatient and lashed out at another because you were really worried or angry at someone else?

Never   Seldom   Sometimes   Often

37. Do you feel shame for staying in a relationship and putting up with troublesome behavior with another for so long but are afraid to drop the relationship?

Never   Seldom   Sometimes   Often

38. Do others accuse you of taking things too seriously?

Never   Seldom   Sometimes   Often

39. Do others accuse you of being too impatient, critical or demanding?

Never   Seldom   Sometimes   Often

40. Do you make extra efforts to please others because it is very important that they accept you personally and won't reject you?

Never   Seldom   Sometimes   Often

Looking at your responses, any "Often" responses are an issue and worth investigating – perhaps with a therapist. If you have a pattern of frequent "Often" responses – then therapy is definitely in order. The more your responses lean in that direction, the more attention is worthy.

On the other hand, if your pattern is "Never" or leaning toward "Never," all is well and good. Congratulations – IF YOU HAVE BEEN HONEST WITH YOURSELF.

Your power. Stop giving it away.

1. Understanding Personal Power

As we begin, we need to make sure we are all speaking the same language and using the same terminology. We can't talk about the currency of power – the acquiring, accumulating, saving, spending or squandering – until we define the word "power." For each of us, power is "The ability to get what I want." Power currencies are how we earn, spend, save or unfortunately squander that power.

Do you feel like you are getting what you want in your life? Too often, that's just not true. Most of us struggle to get what we want – or what we *think* we want – but fall short.

Powerful people get what they want. That's the point. So how do they do that? That's the concept we need to fully analyze and understand.

How is it that some people seem to dominate a situation and others do not? Why are some so capable of the movement of events and dictating their outcomes while others lack that power and are relegated to the sidelines? What have they got that we don't have, and how are they using it so effectively?

Ideally, the ability to get what we want should be something we learn at an early age and perfect as we mature. But in reality, it seems to be quite the opposite. The foundation for developing power begins at infancy. I've learned from my research that most of us do not master empowerment early on. As children, we are quite egocentric, which is actually appropriate for certain developmental stages. An infant needs to know and more fully define the "self" before he or she can successfully interact with others.

It is not only appropriate for small children to be egocentric; it is essential. As babies, without knowing the words to use, we wonder "Who am I? What are my limitations? What is a foot? What is a nose? How do I use them?" These are foundational learnings that help us build a more comprehensive sense of self that can be applied to family situations and other interactions. Mastering our attributes and functions is that starting point. As we grow older, we learn more sophisticated interpersonal techniques.

One of the first instincts that a newborn child has is to cry, and children learn quickly that crying gets some results. Crying, when it is all one has, can be an effective way of achieving desired results. If a child cries because of an uncomfortable sensation, that often results in a new diaper. The child quickly learns that there was discomfort before and crying gained improvement of the situation. Sometimes that child will cry and get fed or burped instead of a diaper change. In that instance, crying did not get the desired outcome, or it took longer to get a diaper change. Over time, the child learns how others react to crying and how it can satisfy basic needs. At that stage in life, crying is an effective power currency. Put that in the infant's power currency "bank account."

A newborn child has an extremely limited repertoire of activities and skills aimed at getting what she or he wants. That's a very limited measure of empowerment, but it is the beginning of understanding the dynamics of power. Once we get to the terrible twos and the troublesome threes, interactions become more complex. Children discover that temper tantrums – a heightened form of crying – can be a useful tool in their power repertoire. True, it can gain some kind of response, but the response may not be the one desired. Depending on the recipient, a tantrum may result in punishment, the exact opposite of what was desired. As the toddler grows and develops, the child can learn that many factors come into play when trying to use their newfound power of the temper tantrum.

Parents respond differently to tantrums, and that often depends on their mood, the location of the tantrum (like the grocery store) and their own experiences as children. We know all parents who often give in to temper tantrums – meaning they do what the child wants – just to make it stop. My research has shown that it is usually inadequate parenting and only reinforces the use of the tantrum, thus insuring its repeated performance in the future. Plus, the parents are squandering the power needed to gain proper behavior from the child instead of tantrums. The parent has thereby taught the child that tantrums work, so why not use them?

With appropriate parenting, the child grows to learn more sophisticated and suitable interpersonal techniques and avoids the need to unlearn behaviors that rob the child of its power. As children age, they learn quickly that the way they "spent their power currency" in their own family context will impact how they "invest their power" in the world outside the family.

We all can cite observations of how children, teens and even adults test various forms of power during their developmental stages, with varied success. When we look at that process, it is one of trial and error, power "well-spent" and power "squandered." Was it beneficial in the long run or wasted for a range of reasons?

Substandard role-modeling by parents inhibits a child's ability to develop optimally. When parents lack the skills of effective empowerment, the kind of role model they provide their children leaves the child with inferior skills going forward. They are not fully prepared for "the real world" because they have not learned how to effectively accumulate (earn), save (think about locking away in a vault), spend (or use) or squander (splurge) their power currency.

Another substantial reason is the values of our culture. When "the system" advocates for highly ineffective empowerment methods and teaches children to adopt to those methods, they are ill equipped for their futures.

Going back to our definition, power is "The ability to get what I want." It sounds simple, but I think we can all agree that most of us fail to get what we want.

By and large, most people think wealth is the primary method to acquire what they want. As a result, they spend their days in the fervent attempt to amass wealth, much to the abandonment of more rewarding activities, and only with marginal success.

Being wealthy has an impact to be sure, but as this analysis unfolds, we will see why wealth alone does not yield the kind of effectiveness to true and lasting empowerment. "You can't buy happiness," is a standard motto.

You've also heard the phrase "more money, more problems," which is the opposite of what most people want when they finally gain wealth. They think everything will be better, but that's a fool's folly. The problems are just different or on a grander scale. Wealth empowers in limited ways, on a limited basis, and only as long as the wealth exists. It's incredibly finite. When an economy crashes and the wealth disappears, those who built their empowerment on a financial basis alone are much worse off. They have squandered their personal power. We will see that wealth makes weak and shallow promises that do not empower in effective ways in a larger scale and over time.

The same can be true for other traditional methods of amassing power such as appearance, fame, athletic prowess and even attention on social media. In so many ways, we have built a culture on "bankrupt" values and empty promises that do not work effectively, nor do they endure.

"The ability to get what I want" – the way it is approached today – usually frustrates more than it inspires. What percent of the population will ever become wealthy? What percent of the population will have outstanding good looks or be famous or impress the world as superior athletes or social media "influencers?" The answer is – an extremely small percentage. When we buy into that, which is what our culture entices us to do, we squander our power and set ourselves up for failure.

Our focus on those superficial aspects of life causes most of us to diminish our power. We remain ineffective practitioners of power. But it doesn't have to be that way. We don't have to accept the status quo. This book will show you how to better acquire personal power, save it for appropriate uses, spend it in effective ways and avoid squandering it.

Power Currency! How to Stop Squandering and Start Increasing Your Personal Power uses financial terms to convey the principles of personal power because that's something we all understand. We all know how to earn, save, spend and squander money. In this book you will learn how to do the same with your own personal power: How we earn it, save it, spend it, and avoid squandering it, in order to gain the most benefit – to get what we want!

Once you understand these concepts, you can apply them to your life and build your own "personal power portfolio." Who doesn't want to build a growing, diversified portfolio of personal power that you can use to get what you want? The wonderful thing is that we can build that power portfolio no matter our actual financial status. Once we build the portfolio, we will see that power is not just about material wealth. When we dive deep into its understandings and gain that solid foundation, we may find that we are getting what we want even more than we expected.

At the end of each chapter there are questions designed to encourage you to think about your own "power portfolio." These are to inspire you to think differently so that by the end of the book, you are comfortable and ready to start building your power enhancement.

Building A Power Portfolio

- What kind of discipline did your parents use to get you to behave?
    - What impact did that have on you?
    - What did you learn from it that you applied to your own situation or your own children?
- What do you see as the main means of power our culture advocates?
    - Are these ones that will endure no matter what?
- What kinds of ambitions get reinforced in our present culture?
    - What are the consequences?
    - Are they always positive?
    - How do we mismanage our power?
- What do you wish our culture would advocate as rewarding

ambitions?

- ◦ How can we lead our lives to effect that change?

2. Earning Power Currency

There are a variety of reasons we do not get what we want. First among them is the poor choice of "power currency."

By definition, a "power currency" is an action/event or attitude/belief that contributes to our power account. Think of them as pennies, nickels, dimes and dollars that add up as they are deposited. Some things have very little power, so they have less value, like loose change. Others have a great deal of power, similar to a bonus at work or winning millions with Publisher's Clearinghouse. Some have only short-term power; others are enduring.

Here is a list of power currencies: Education, Kindness, Job Title, Politeness, Authority, Appreciation, Manipulation, Pleasant Appearance, Coercion, Cheerfulness, Selfishness, Considerate of Others, Anger/Threats, Helpfulness, Stereotyping, Accepting, Stubborn, Flexible/Easy Going.

As a former Boy Scout, I would add: Trustworthy, Loyal, Helpful, Friendly, Courteous, Kind, Obedient, Thrifty, Brave, Clean and Reverent.

To understand the value of each of these "power currencies," think about what you observe regarding people you know or encounter and how they go about trying to get what they want. Think about how they use their "power currencies" and the results they get – positive or negative.

In my research, people typically identify words like bully, controlling, loud, manipulative, wealth, seniority, stubborn, threats, gossip, fear, distrust, physical strength and fame when naming tactics people use to get things their way. And I also hear things like trustworthy, dedicated, hardworking, knowledgeable, thoughtful, caring and respected.

When this list is given in the context of an organization or a family system to generate an awareness of what is commonly and, to some extent, effectively used by individuals to gain that they want, it is an enlightening window into their personal interactions and the culture of that system.

Even more fascinating is why some behavior is tolerated while other is not, but we will address that later.

So, why aren't we all getting what we want all the time? Why aren't we properly managing our power accounts to maximize results?

Valuation check: There are actually two types of power currency; **short term** and **long term**. By definition, a short-term power currency means "the more I use it, the less likely I am to get what I want." A long-term power currency means "the more I use it, the more likely I am to get what I want."

Short-term power may be effective, but it is not lasting. It's like making an impulse purchase at a store. You are excited at first and then realize it's an item you didn't really need. Long-term power currency almost always grows and maintains its effectiveness and value. It's a "better investment" – like a solid blue-chip stock over a risky IPO.

Think of it this way: "The more I use a short-term power currency, the more it wears out and becomes less effective – and often even becomes counter-effective." That's something you probably didn't even consider. Like the impulse purchase, a short-term currency may even lead to regret.

Consequently, "The more I use a long-term power currency, the better I am enabled to get what I want, and it will last longer." Like a good investment that continues to steadily gain in value, long-term currency historically provides a greater return.

Let's go back to the list of power currencies. Now that we know the difference, which list is short-term, and which is long-term?

All these items are short term – education, job title, authority, manipulation, coercion, selfishness, anger/threats, stereotyping, stubborn. Let's explore each of them to get a better understanding.

Education – I am Doctor Lehr. If I constantly remind you that I am Doctor Lehr, I may be implying that I am superior and therefore entitled to get what I want. However, there is a consequence to this action. You are more inclined to push back because my education does not concern or impress you. So, I have offended you with my short-term power currency.

Job Title – Likewise, if I am your boss and repeatedly remind you that you must do what I tell you to do and lord it over you, you are likely to become resentful. So again, my power is squandered in a short-term power currency. It is not lasting and will result in my being an ineffective boss.

Understanding these differences means that we can apply the concept to our own situations. There may be times when a short-term power currency is all we need, or all we are able to "afford," which may work in a particular situation. For example, while I was director of the outpatient mental health department at a hospital, if we wanted something from another department, I'd ask my administrative assistant to contact that other department and make the request. If she got a "no," I'd make the request myself. And I would get, "Oh, Doctor Lehr, sure we can do that." While an administrative assistant got a "no," the department head got a "yes," so being a boss or in a high-management position or having a title can have power in certain situations. But when that power currency is used too much, the account gets depleted, and people get tired of being "ordered around."

Manipulation – I may be able to manipulate you once, possibly even twice. But the third time I try to manipulate you to get what I want, then it will likely fail.

The same goes for **coercion, selfishness, anger/threats** and **stubbornness**. They all lose their effectiveness in the short term. People get tired of these attempts by others to get what they want, and that currency is soon depleted, or loses its value, and is rendered ineffective. The account is once again empty and even in danger of an overdraft.

To consistently use short-term power currency as a means of getting what one wants is to squander one's power, which is exactly what we don't want to do. The key to short-term power currency is to spend it or use it judiciously because it cannot be sustained.

Yet our society lauds qualities like wealth, fame, physical

adeptness, cunning and even manipulation. We admire those who gain by such shallow means. At least for a while.

Fame is not enduring unless it is backed by genuine talent and competence, and even then it depends on a notoriously fickle audience whose attention can be fleeting. An actor or actress is famous only as long as he/she continues to produce outstanding performances. Once the top quality is no longer on display, the fame can quickly disappear.

The same is true for wealth. The 2008 financial recession ought to have taught us not to depend on wealth for our long-term confidence. Wealth can vanish quickly – and that is beyond our control. None of us loses wealth on purpose. Wealth is important – that is obvious. But if we are solely dependent, or overly dependent, on wealth to get us what we want, we are misguided and limiting ourselves. We are putting all our power investments in one stock instead of diversifying.

Anger and threats – quickly lose their power.

Stereotyping – is an interesting one. Stereotyping as a power currency functions by separating people into the "acceptable" group and the "unacceptable" group – the "us" versus "them." We are better than they are – often on very shallow and false merit.

However, the more one investigates a stereotype, the more it fails to hold up. All of "them" do not fit any stereotype. And if *all* of "them" do not fit, then the stereotype does not succeed. It fails in the face of the facts. Thus, stereotyping is an ineffective means to gain power and influence.

Let me be clear: short-term power currencies are effective – *for the short term*. They do work, but only for a while and for a price. Eventually they lose their effectiveness, squander our power, compromise our ability to achieve influence and deprive of us what we want.

Many of the short-term power currencies exist precisely because of their limited efficacy. We are seduced by the short-term gains and fail to measure the longer-term consequences to our overall power portfolio. We lose sight of the big picture.

Bolstered by short-term success, some use these power currencies until they are exhausted, and they are left with no backup, no nest egg to fall back on.

Now let's examine the remainder of the power currency list – kindness, politeness, appreciation, pleasant appearance, cheerfulness, considerate of others, helpfulness, accepting, flexible/easy going.

Who gets tired of **kindness**? When does **politeness** lose its charm? And who doesn't like **appreciation**? Who doesn't value **cheerfulness**? And who doesn't want to be **accepted** rather than ignored or judged?

And existing in a more **flexible** setting is far more comfortable than one that is strictly rigid and unbending. An **easy-going** friend is usually appreciated more than one who is compulsively overbearing and tightly controlling.

When we seek to get what we want using short-term power currency, we squander our power, diminish its effectiveness and minimize its value and influence.

However, when we use long-term currency, we maximize our effectiveness, increase our value and influence and gain an enhanced ability to get what we want.

I mentioned the Mid-Atlantic Association for Training and Consulting in my introduction. That is where I was taught this important perspective. I attended a one-week event on power utilization and conflict management. There were about 40 of us – mostly mental health professionals – at the training. Part of the experience was to evaluate each other to determine who were the more influential and effective practitioners of power among the group.

Early in the week, one lady was identified as powerful. And as the week progressed, her power continued to grow. This kind and gentle lady started the week by getting to know each of the other participants by asking: Who are you? Why are you at this training? What do you hope to learn? And how can I be of assistance? She was not intrusive, but humble and caring. The warmth of her character and compassion were evident. And if she were to ask me to do something for her, I would gladly assent.

As the week went on, we grew to trust her even more. We were convinced that she would not take advantage of us, and she was dedicated to our success even as to her own. She was the real deal, and we afforded her respect and confidence. And she was truly powerful in all the right kinds of ways.

That is a clear example of someone who was rightfully earning her power currency by "investing" her positive qualities – warmth and compassion – and thus "spending" those qualities on the group. Her impact on us was lasting; a long-term power currency.

Yet as a culture, we covet the short-term. We are a *consumerist culture!* The key phrases for this culture are: Why should I? What's in it for me? What am I going to get out of it? What's it going to cost me? Everything is new and improved! Be the first on your block! Be the envy of all your friends! Have it your way... Get more. Pay less.

And on and on we are indoctrinated by advertising and various forms of media that bombard us daily. This is the predominate theme of our consumerist culture. *It's all about me!*

Well if it is all about *me*, then aggression, selfishness, greed and all of that become the norm. These are all obviously short-term power currencies. The very culture that surrounds us indoctrinates us into the pattern of short-term power currency. That can be difficult to see past, but with the proper tools, it can be done.

We squander our power by giving in to the directions and values of this *consumerist culture* that does not serve us for the long term.

Focusing solely on our wants and needs isolates us from others and deprives us of their support, assistance, encouragement, companionship, ideas and suggestions. We need to learn to resist and present another perspective for more successful living.

Building A Power Portfolio

- Brainstorm a list of the power currencies generally used by those with whom you work or associate.

- Are they long-term or short-term?
- Can you tell the difference?
- Do the same, honest, brainstorming exercise for yourself.
  - What do you use to generally get what you want?
  - Are you using long-term or short-term methods?
  - How effective are your methods over time?
- Think about the education system.
  - Are we preparing our children to know the difference between long-term and short-term currency?
  - What could we do better?
- Consider our politicians.
  - Are they using long-term or short-term power currency in their efforts?
  - What are the consequences?

3. Balancing Self-Interest

In the last chapter, we learned how we diminish our power by using the wrong power currencies. Now let's explore the **concept of self-interest**. Specifically, "What is my self-interest?"

First, we need to use the same concept as before by dividing our self-interests into **two major categories – long-term self-interest** and **short-term self-interest.**

Either a self-interest is designed to meet your immediate needs (short-term) or the self-interest is designed to meet your longer-term needs. In brief, is it for *now* (short-term) or is it for *later* (my long-term benefit)?

An example for me would be cheesecake. I really like cheesecake. I would eat cheesecake all the time if I could (short-term self-interest). However, I also weigh more than I would like. So not indulging in cheesecake as much as I would like is in my long-term self-interest. Having cheesecake on special occasions satisfies my short-term self-interests and resisting the temptation at other times fits my long-term self-interest to have a healthy body.

I can say the same for many fatty foods that taste really great. Do I really need to eat them? What benefit do I gain from eating them other than immediate gratification? Would it be better for me to abstain, or at least reserve such treats for only special occasions?

Let's look at another example. When a colleague makes a cutting and inappropriate remark about me, I can choose how to respond. I can immediately berate the colleague strongly using harsh language and thus gain some sense of retribution, or I can use a more diplomatic manner: "That remark didn't make me feel good. Did you mean to be so hurtful?"

By being more controlled, I invite the colleague into a dialog that has the promise of a positive resolution for the both of us. Giving in to the emotions of the moment can give me a sense of release and immediate gratification (short-term), but often that may only make matters worse later (long-term).

In learning to identify short- and long-term self-interests, we develop the skill of reflecting before we speak or act which will ultimately contribute to our long-term self-interest and our power account. Yes, what my colleague said was inappropriate and offensive. That is a fact – that is, **if** I heard it and understood it correctly. There is always the possibility of jumping to conclusions or not understanding someone's actions. That's another benefit of the long-term option. It provides an opportunity to clarify the situation before deciding on a response – which avoids an episode of squandering my power needlessly.

If I understood the remark correctly and it was meant to be out of line, then I have choices. Short-term = harsh and challenging rebuke. Long-term = invite the colleague into dialog that can diminish the situation and gain a healthier relationship for the long run.

One big concept of long-term versus short-term self-interests is learning to develop the skill of internally reflecting before we speak or act. Indeed, what my colleague said may have been offensive, but I have the power to decide how I want to respond. Helpful response or hurtful response? Just because I have been offended does not mean I need to offend in return.

As you can imagine, this concept takes practice to develop. It does not come naturally for most of us. We want to hurt back when we are hurt, similar to the temper tantrum we learned as children. When we are hit, either physically or emotionally, we want to hit back. But that instinct is only in our short-term self-interest and may not be benefit us at all in the long term.

Taking the time to reflect in a situation and ask ourselves, "Is this in my long-term self-interest or am I giving in to a short-term response?" is a chip that will raise the value of our personal power portfolio. Building up our long-term self-interest will not only teach us to make smart choices, it will empower us for future challenges. This concept applies to not just our words, but our actions as well.

When faced with these choices, and we ask ourselves, "If I do 'X' will it merely meet my short-term self-interest or is it consistent with my long-term personal power goals?

There is another aspect to this. It is a **paradox** that **the more one hoards power, the less powerful one becomes. And the more one empowers, the more powerful one becomes.**

Let me illustrate it this way. Early in my career I worked under a very controlling boss. He was extremely dedicated to his work and very much wanted the enterprise to succeed. He isolated himself in his office, diligently explored all the options ahead for our work, and then dictated what we should do.

The boss went to team meetings and explained his process. He then told us what was best for us and the company and ordered us to do it. Needless to say, my co-workers did not warm up to this boss; most felt like he was demeaning (though perhaps unintentionally).

Then our boss was stricken with a serious heart attack and was out of commission for some months. As his "next in command," I had to assume the duties of directing the operation. I was fresh out of graduate school and knew I had some ideas, but they had not been seriously tested in real life.

So instead of going to the team meetings and telling everyone what to do as our boss had done, I simply said, "Listen gang, I don't have a clue. What do you think?"

I invited my colleagues into the decision-making process. Together we made good decisions, and the dedication to fulfill those decisions increased. By functioning in that collaborative way, I empowered all the staff to have a voice and a certain amount of control. Morale rose and output increased.

The downside was that the staff began to say, "We like the young guy better than the old guy." Oops! My intent was not to subvert the authority of the boss, but simply to do the job the best way I knew how.

To hoard power is to diminish or squander one's power. To empower – to encourage and enable others to claim their power and participate in the decision-making and implementation of those ideas gives them a greater sense of ownership and commitment to the outcome.

This applies not only to the work environment, but to a full range of situations.

Parenting: as my children grew older and were mature enough to assume responsibilities, my wife and I sought to empower them to help make family decisions.

A side part of that – if my child wanted something that might be expensive, my immediate reaction might be to say "no," but instead I would say, "Yes, you can have that when..." You may have that when you save enough money to buy it, or you may have that when you do some extra chores around the house, so Mom and Dad don't have to do everything. Get the idea? I tried to rarely say "no." I tried instead to model for my children that they can have what they want by using their own power. They could make it happen. It did not need to be given to them. They could have some responsibility in earning it and thus increase the value of the object or opportunity, unwittingly enhancing their long-term personal power accounts.

Long-term versus short-term self-interest is an incredibly valuable concept. When mastered and used wisely it will save us from making poor decisions or doing things that squander our power and deplete our power account in the long run. And it enables us to move forward in directions that will have a better chance for us to gain what we truly want.

To hoard power is to diminish or "spend" our ability to get what we want. To empower is to maximize our chance to increase our power accounts and get what we truly want.

Now that we understand the concept of self-interest, let's explore the root of self-interest by learning to identify what we truly want or need.

I am a spiritual person – in fact, an ordained pastor in the Lutheran church.

After at least 40 years of testing and evaluating, I finally discovered what were effectively my long-term self-interests. There are two: 1. To ever mature more deeply in my faith and my relationship with the Holy (to become more spiritually mature); and 2. To like the person I see in the mirror (to lay claim to my self-esteem and feel good about myself).

I would assert that by seeking those two long-term goals I will be a better person, husband, father, grandfather, (and now even great-grandfather), neighbor, friend, colleague and all the rest. I can measure every opportunity of what I say or what I do according to those two standards. Will this enrich my spiritual maturity? Will I like the person I see in the mirror? Those two qualifications can guide all the rest of my life.

To break it down, I made a list of what was important to me. Once I realized that many of the items were either redundant or comparable, I was able to narrow it down to two main items. I identified them as the two most important stocks in my personal power portfolio. I would continue investing in those stocks, for the long-term, to build my personal power.

Clearly, to be wealthy or attractive or athletic or all those things the world continually suggests are the path to power – to getting what one wants – are not what I discerned as effective. Wealth can come and go. As I write this, the experts are predicting a recession in the next few years. I lost a ton of money in the 2008 recession through no fault of my own.

Being attractive – that wanes with the years. I don't want to make a bad appearance, but personal beauty is not my quest.

Athletic – try that when you are in your 70's like me. I'm just glad some days that I can make it up the stairs. I do attempt to exercise regularly to remain fit. I highly advocate fitness. Fitness is in my long-term self-interest. I like looking in the mirror and seeing someone who is fit.

All those concepts the world proposes are usually not durable or lasting. They are, at best, short-term self-interests and do not pass the test of time. Seek instead the long-term self-interests that will endure in ways that enhance our wellness and wellbeing physically, emotionally/mentally, and spiritually. We are holistic creatures and need to be sustained and equipped for life in a holistic way that enhances our power accounts and enriches us for all that can come our way.

In addition, who can deprive me of a greater spiritual maturity or my own self-esteem? There is no outside force that can strip either of those from me. I am in complete control with my spiritual devotion and development as well as my self-worth and self-esteem.

No one can take from me my spiritual maturity or self-esteem, so that means I possess all the power I will ever need to fulfill my own long-term self-interests. And that's no small deal!

Here's another perspective. Jackie French Koller said, "There are two ways of being rich, if by rich we mean having everything we want. One way is to amass a fortune and purchase everything we want. The other way to be rich, to have everything we want, is to want very little."

True example: We have a friend who, in her early adult years, could put everything she owned in a shopping bag. She worked in non-profit work and did not need much for her life. Her long-term goal is to get back to the point where everything she owns will fit into a shopping bag. Realistically, how many pairs of shoes do we need? How many sweaters, shirts, pants, etc.? We can wash our clothes frequently and not need a large wardrobe. It is a matter of priorities and values. Do we value practicality and frugality? Or do we value vanity and public appearance? What is in our long-term self-interest? To spend lots of money on fashion, or to invest our means in things more lasting?

Now let me be clear, I am not advocating severe austerity. What our friend did is an extreme. I cite it merely as an example of what one person did. For me, I seek a reasonable and modest lifestyle that is not extravagant or plush. Perhaps the term "moderation" fits? Adequate, while making room in our finances for generous contributions to charities, is my goal. If we sell out the charities to afford a luxurious lifestyle, that would be counter to my long-term self-interests. There's nothing spiritually mature about that kind of self-centered attitude.

Another perspective: The rock group Queen sings, "I want it all, I want it all, I want it all, and I want it now!" This accurately reflects the consumerist attitudes of our current culture. It's all about me! Based on our self-interest discussions, that attitude is not in our long-term self-interest.

Another point of focus is that self-interest and selfishness are not the same. It is important to note the distinction. It is almost never in our long-term self-interest to live life selfishly. That often only isolates us and pushes others away in the solo pursuit of our own short-term interests. So selfish is not a long-term self-interest.

One more perspective: We have been focusing on personal self-interests, but the concept can be expanded. There are also corporate self-interests. Families have long-term self-interests as a unit. Organizations have long-term self-interests. Businesses have long-term self-interests. Too often on the corporate/group level, we fail to take the time to measure short-term versus long-term self-interests. And that leads us away from any genuine success, thereby squandering our power.

No one can take from me my spiritual maturity or my self-esteem. I am endowed with all the power I will ever need – so long as I don't squander it on short-term self-interests.

Building A Power Portfolio

- What are your long-term self-interests?
  - If you don't know, how can you discern them?
  - Conversations with others on a similar quest will help.
- What are the usual short-term self-interests that bombard you regularly?
  - How can you gain control over them?
  - Who can assist you?
  - Who will hold you accountable?
- What are the long-term self-interests of your family or your organization?

- ◦ How were they determined?
- ◦ Was it a collaborative process?
- ◦ Who "owns" those long-term self-interests?
- Do you understand how hoarding power squanders the ability to get what you want?
  - ◦ How can you more effectively empower those in your life as a means of enhancing your own power?

4. Investing Your Personal Power

For this chapter, I need to give credit to several authorities in the field; Dr. Donald Hands, in Wisconsin; Anne Wilson Schaef, Co-dependence: Misunderstood and Mistreated (Harper, San Francisco, 1986); and Schaef along with Diane Fassel, The Addictive Organization (Harper, San Francisco, 1988), The Johnson Institute. I have taken their work along with others and adapted it with my own approach.

Codependence comes from the addictions field. We suppose a family that consists of Mom, Dad, Junior and Sis. Dad is a drunk. For Dad to be an addict and remain active in the family, Mom, Junior and Sis all have to be codependent – they have to cooperate with the addiction as enablers. It is that enabling – going along and not seriously resisting – that is the codependence.

As with any terms we use, it is prudent to provide a definition. This is how I define codependence.

A set of maladaptive learned behaviors that a person uses to survive when experiencing great emotional pain and stress and that are passed on from generation to generation. These behaviors and their accompanying attitudes are self-defeating and result in diminished capacity. Codependents typically do not take adequate care of themselves and are far too controlled by (or controlling of) other persons' behaviors and attitudes.

Codependent characteristics include but are not limited to care-taking, low self-worth, obsession, control, denial, difficulty having fun, loyalty, sharing, dependency, boundary violations or boundary confusion, mistrust, anger, inappropriate sexuality, inappropriate intimacy and indirect communication.

Now some of these behaviors seem quite noble, like loyalty or sharing. The issue is, to what extent? Loyalty is grand until it goes too far and is self-defeating. Likewise, sharing is good until it is at a cost that amounts to self-deprivation. This is where limits, boundaries and fairness come into play.

Let me illustrate with my codependence graph adapted from the work of Donald Hands.

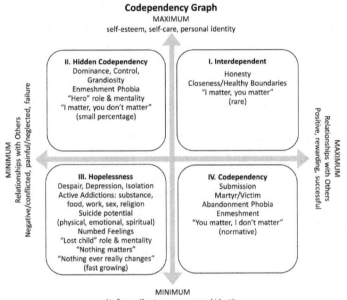

Codependency Graph

MAXIMUM
self-esteem, self-care, personal identity

II. Hidden Codependency
Dominance, Control,
Grandiosity
Enmeshment Phobia
"Hero" role & mentality
"I matter, you don't matter"
(small percentage)

I. Interdependent
Honesty
Closeness/Healthy Boundaries
"I matter, you matter"
(rare)

III. Hopelessness
Despair, Depression, Isolation
Active Addictions: substance,
food, work, sex, religion
Suicide potential
(physical, emotional, spiritual)
Numbed Feelings
"Lost child" role & mentality
"Nothing matters"
"Nothing ever really changes"
(fast growing)

IV. Codependency
Submission
Martyr/Victim
Abandonment Phobia
Enmeshment
"You matter, I don't matter"
(normative)

MINIMUM Relationships with Others
Negative/conflicted, painful/neglected, failure

MAXIMUM Relationships with Others
Positive, rewarding, successful

MINIMUM
No/low self-esteem, no personal identity
Lack of self-care/personal neglect

The graph has two intersecting lines. A vertical line goes from top (maximum self-care, self-esteem, and personal identity) to the bottom (minimum self-care, self-esteem, and personal identity). The horizontal line goes from right (maximum relationships with others that are positive, rewarding, and successful) to the left (minimum relationships with others that are negative, conflicted, painful, neglected, and failing). This then renders four quadrants.

The four quadrants of the codependency graph are numbered: I, II, III, IV.

Quadrant I: Interdependent – This quadrant represents the characteristics of honesty with self and with others; closeness while maintaining healthy physical and emotional boundaries; and an "I matter, and you matter" attitude. This is a win/win quadrant that seeks good collaboration when involved with others in an open and sincere fashion. Interdependent values begin with respect for self as well as respect for all others. This quadrant is very rare, especially in organizations – but more on that later.

Interdependent is the healthy quadrant identified as maximum self-care, self-esteem, and a well-formed and mature personal identity. The people in this quadrant know honestly and fully who they are as opposed to who they are not. They accept who they are while appropriately addressing our faults and failures. In addition, people in Quadrant I enjoy healthy and rewarding relationships with others that are positive and gratifying. They understand the concept of healthy boundaries which are respected and maintained both for self and for others.

Quadrant II: Hidden Codependency – People in this quadrant are attempting to maintain maximum self-care, only in a more toxic form. Concern for healthy relationships with others does not matter. These individuals are more interested in dominance and control of others, assuming this will enhance their own self-esteem and status. "Hidden Codependence" means they depend on others to play along and allow the perpetrator to dominate and rescue.

Quadrant II has the characteristics of dominance, control, grandiosity, enmeshment phobia (god forbid I become like them!) and a "hero" mentality (rescuing others from their mediocrity). It is an "I matter, you don't matter" approach that is self-defeating. Remember that to hoard power is to diminish power. To empower (as in Quadrant I) is to gain power. Quadrant II is an "I win, you lose" attitude.

Quadrant II is a kind of personality cult – "I alone have the answers to your problems. I alone can save you from your troubles. I alone..." And when the constituents comply with someone asserting that dominance, it creates a personality cult and all that goes with it. Power to the people is zero. Power is limited to the one in control who presents a false sense of strength that lasts only as long as the constituents agree to be dominated. As soon as the constituents assert their own power, the dominance crumbles.

Quadrant II is not satisfying and wears out quickly in any group or organizational setting. Managers who function in this manner find a low loyalty among those whom they manage. They are simply bullies, and who likes a bully? Sooner or later the constituents realize that their "hero" is fallible and not dependable, and the jig is up.

Quadrant III: Hopelessness – This quadrant is characterized by a state of quitting, giving up and/or deciding that it's just not worth the effort anymore. People in this quadrant have abandoned good self-care, self-esteem and no longer hold a healthy personal identity. They have also given up on interpersonal relationships they find overwhelming or terribly disappointing.

The primary characteristics are despair, depression and isolation. There arises the possibility of addiction with drugs, food, sex and even work and religion (religion used all the wrong ways). They seek ways to "medicate" for the loneliness and pain of life in this quadrant. The overwhelming feelings of physical, emotional (going numb) and spiritual hopelessness can even result in suicidal tendencies. These people choose to just turn off their feelings because they are so disturbing (going numb). They have a sense of being a "lost child" for whom no one cares or even notices. It gets to the point that nothing matters – they've tried all kinds of solutions and nothing seems to work. They finally resign to the fact that nothing will ever change and surrender their ability to make a difference (lose power). This is a fast-growing quadrant, a lose/lose attitude.

Quadrant IV: Codependency – These individuals have sacrificed self-care, self-esteem, and a strong and healthy personal identity for the sake of relationships with others. Here the primary characteristics are submission, assuming the role of martyr or victim, abandonment phobia (god forbid they might reject me), enmeshment (personal identity lost in the submission), and the attitude that "you matter, and I don't matter" or you win, I lose.

Clearly one's person power and influence are sacrificed for the sake of popularity and acceptance. One squanders power by trying to please everyone else. It is constantly demanding and exhausting. And eventually it builds resentment. "Why am I giving so much and getting so little in return?" People will often take advantage of someone who is too willingly submissive. "If you want to be my servant, go ahead. I'll take advantage of that any time." That is a frequent response to classic codependency. Don't ask the other to change or be appropriately responsible, just do it all yourself to the point of being depleted and upset. "Why don't others respect me and treat me better?" The answer is because you don't respect yourself or insist on being treated fairly.

This is the place where many people gravitate due to the pressures of family, work and society. Our culture seeks to put us all in the "you win, I lose" position based on a lack of self-esteem. Because people don't have the strength to stand up for themselves, others take what they can get from that dependence. No one wants to be rejected. So, these people inappropriately diminish themselves believing that it will earn status and recognition when in reality, all it gets them is disregard and abuse. But that is a profound aspect of our culture everyone should understand. It rewards Quadrant IV behavior. "What a lovely suffering servant you are!" Here is where these people get their atta-boys and atta-girls. They capitulate to the pressures to comply and be subservient.

Those who land in Quadrant IV usually find it exhausting and unsatisfying. "Why do we give so much and get so little?" This builds resentment, and that resentment turns to disgust. Disgust turns to discontent. And discontent turns to anger. "It just isn't fair!"

Often, these people take their anger and shift to Quadrant II and seek to "take control" and demand their rights over others, which will only meet with resistance and rejection. Folks will not tolerate a bully very long. It is an extremely short-term self-interest and a very poor power currency.

Having failed in Quadrants IV and II, these people sink to Quadrant III and just give up. "It's just not worth it. I quit. I yield. Who cares? I'll just put my life in cruise control."

They surrender to the pressures from family and work and society and abandon their own self-interests just to survive – or so they believe.

This is powerlessness at its extreme. Hopelessness, despair and depression are the depths of power utilization. They are withdrawn from themselves and into an abyss of capitulation.

Please note: the movement from Quadrant IV to Quadrant I has very little to do with how we treat others. It has everything to do with how we treat ourselves and how we allow others to treat us. Sustaining our own self-esteem has nothing to do with others. There's the big mistake.

When we depend on others for our self-esteem, we are in Quadrant IV – dependent. When we stand on our own and affirm for ourselves our self-worth and self-esteem, we are Interdependent and demonstrate a strong self-identity that is healthy and firm and eager to engage with others.

Let me give a profound example. This comes from the work of Viktor Frankl (Man's Search for Meaning, Touchstone Book, 1984).

Frankl was a detainee in a Nazi concentration camp during WWII. If hell ever had a mailing address, such places would qualify.

Frankl noticed that most of the detainees walked around with their heads down and shoulders bent. They manifested the logical despair that such places inspired. If this is a good day, we will only be tortured and abused. If it is a bad day, it is our turn to be killed. So, understandably, many existed in utter hopelessness and despair.

However, Frankl also observed that some detainees walked around with their heads up and their backs erect. Those were the ones who knew the truth. "Yes, you can abuse me and torture me if you want. You can even kill me. Then all you will have is my dead body. BUT you cannot take my self-esteem from me unless I give it to you."

This is an important concept and one everyone should repeat until it is seared into their consciousness: NO ONE CAN TAKE YOUR SELF-ESTEEM OR YOUR SELF-WORTH UNLESS YOU GIVE IT TO THEM!!

That is a profound and eternal truth. That is a powerful truth. That is an empowering truth. And those who lay claim to that truth know the meaning of personal power.

NO ONE can take from us our self-esteem, our personal identity or our self-worth unless we give it to them. It is ours. It is not theirs to control or to determine. It is personal and it is within our control and only our control.

Frankl's observation is one of the best examples of giving one's power away or not.

Move from whatever quadrant you are in into Quadrant I and discover what it means to have personal power. Do not let others, or the work, or the boss or any other entity have dominance over your own self-worth while you affirm the self-worth of others.

Claim it with pride and treat it lovingly. Take care of yourself – body, mind (intellect and emotions) and spirit. Have a healthy lifestyle including what you eat and how you choose to stay active. Stimulate your intellect regularly in whatever way works best for you. And embrace a deep and personal faith in the way you are most comfortable. Being able to manage those elements in your life are the most valuable power currency you will place in your portfolio.

Another perspective on giving our power away is Victim or Victor!

When we are hit with unfortunate circumstances, we can choose to be victims or victors. We can accept the status of victim – woe is me, how sad, how terrible, how unfair, might as well give up, etc.

Or we can rise above the circumstances and choose to be victors – yes, this is challenging, but we can handle it. We can be the master of our own decisions. We can be strong and endure and make the most of any circumstance.

An example: I had a friend who was going blind. It was devastating to her. She saw her life becoming worthless.

I tried to help her find some new meaning in being blind. What challenges will she face? How will she address them and come out a victor? What will this require of her? How will she manage? What resources will she need? Where can she get those resources? What is the next step? And who can be her guide, her companion and assistant?

She had many friends and a devoted husband. They were people of means, not poor. Her ability to rise above the challenge was very good. Yet she chose the "woe is me" attitude that robbed her of her power and confined her to a state of despair and depression. She squandered her power.

In every circumstance, we have the choice how to respond. When we abandon that ownership of the decision, we give our power away.

We should not allow ourselves to be controlled by our circumstances. I grant that some circumstances are enormous and may indeed seem overwhelming, but very, very few are truly insurmountable. It is just that we assign them power over us and give our power away like a blank check.

Even knowing that we have an incurable disease. Okay, we are going to die. Everyone does. Now, how will we choose to spend our last days? How will we embrace death? Will we roll over and give up OR will we be brave and address death as a champion? That is our choice. No one can decide that for us.

Victim or Victor – that is always our call. We need not go to Quadrant III. We need not resign from the challenge. We can embrace it with confidence that whatever it requires, we can do that.

Power – stop giving it away!

Building A Power Portfolio

- With all honesty, which quadrant reflects most of your life? You may be somewhat in one quadrant and also somewhat in another.
  - So, which one is more dominant?
  - What does that mean?
- How successful are you at establishing Quadrant I relationships?
  - What is most challenging about that?
- To what extent are you a victor or a victim generally?

- ○ What caused that?
- Learning from Viktor Frankl, where can you claim more self-esteem and not allow others to take it from you?

5. Squandering Your Power Profits

Two critical ways we squander or diminish our personal power are:

1. We are afraid to use it.
2. We have never been taught or equipped to use it.

Let's start with being afraid.

Some folks will say, "I don't want to upset anybody," "I don't want to cause any trouble" or "I don't want people looking at me or be the center of attention."

These are generally statements that indicate low self-esteem. When we lack the ego strength to stand up for ourselves, we give away our power. Being assertive is our right. If we don't demand what is fair and proper for ourselves, who will?

"I don't want to cause trouble" is an ineffective strategy some people use to gain acceptance. Those people want others to like them because they are not a troublemaker. They are quiet and obedient and believe that will be rewarded with affirmation and inclusion. If it works, they're hanging with the wrong crowd. Those folks don't care about them. They enjoy the opportunity to exert their dominance over others. Anyone in that situation should work to change their behavior. They are in Quadrant IV!

I used the word "assertive" which is different from "aggressive." Assertive is when we appropriately stand for what is decent and right for ourselves in a manner that recognizes and affirms the other's right for what is decent and fair for them. It is a Quadrant I stance, or a win/win posture.

Aggressive is a Quadrant II position that demands what we want regardless how it may impact others. It is an "I win, you lose" assertion. This is the work of a bully. This, we identified, is not in one's long-term self-interest.

Being afraid to call attention to oneself or assert oneself is another method of abandoning one's personal power and will only lead to the frustrations of Quadrant IV. "You win, I lose" is not a position of power. It is a subservient position that shrinks one's power and leaves that person empty and devalued.

Do not be afraid to be assertive and take a stand for what is proper and correct. Someone who is not accustomed to being assertive should use this approach cautiously until they are comfortable and prepared for the possible responses. Do not rush into situations unprepared. Use this method judiciously. Asserting oneself all the time regardless of the situation will demonstrate our poor judgment and will probably not yield the desired results.

Use a mental checklist before reacting to the situation:

- Thoughtfully research the situation
- Evaluate the options and possible circumstances
- Be sure to appreciate the other person's wants and needs
- And then make a stand

Soon this mental checklist will become second nature and part of your power analysis and power portfolio.

Remember your long-term self-interest: Is this what I really need for the kind of person I want to be, or am I giving in to some short-term desires that are not genuine needs?"

Is what I want consistent with my long-term self-interests and does it still allow the other person to pursue their long-term self-interests? If the answer is yes, then stand firm and go for it.

Reminder: As an example, my long-term self-interests are to become ever more mature in my spiritual life and to like the person I see in the mirror. Whatever is consistent and furthers those goals is right and proper, and I should pursue with respect to the other's similar goals. You should periodically remind yourself of your own long-term self-interests. Make sure to stay on track or reassess if necessary.

Let's examine the concept of "never being taught" about personal power.

Let's go back to Mom, Dad, Junior and Sis in the codependence chapter.

Dad clearly has an issue with substance abuse and makes poor short-term self-interest choices. Junior doesn't behave himself, and Dad punishes him. When Junior behaves, Dad still punishes him because he is under the influence and is making poor decisions. How is Junior to learn what it means to stand up for himself?

"Look, I behaved, and I got in trouble. I didn't behave, and I got in trouble. So why bother?" The destructive cycle continues for another generation.

Raised in a family context that mirrors that kind of severe dysfunction strongly inhibits the assimilation of a healthy ego and self-esteem. Junior will first have to acknowledge the burden of such a sad circumstance and do the personal therapy required to heal and gain a healthy and strong ego. He is starting out at an extreme disadvantage as opposed to someone raised in a healthy family environment.

However, family issues are not the only way we learn poor decision making. It occurs in other environments such as school, childcare, neighborhoods, etc. When we are consistently bombarded with information and behaviors that attack and threaten our ego development, we need to address those with intention and consistency. We cannot afford to capitulate.

An axiom we should try to live by is: *To capitulate is to perpetuate*. To give in and simply endure is to accept the injustice and not claim what is rightfully ours.

When one is in such an environment or had been in a threatening setting, it is important to not surrender. The key is to learn to embrace one's own self-worth and be strong. It's not easy, but if we put in the work, the results will be worth it.

Remember Viktor Frankl in Nazi Germany. Even in a place worthy of being called Hell, one can claim their dignity and stand tall.

We do not need to give our power away just because we are afraid to use it or because we have not been taught how to be properly assertive and respectful of our own appropriate needs.

If we hold firm to our long-term self-interests, and if they are properly identified, they will guide us well.

I identified in the definition of codependence that this is passed on from generation to generation. Much of what we learn about self-esteem and power utilization we learn from our parents. Studies show that the most important duty of a parent is to be a healthy role model.

Boys will look to their fathers to determine what it means to be a man, a husband and a father. Girls will look to their mothers to ascertain what it means to be a woman, a wife and a mother.

Of course, children learn important lessons from both parents. Sons look to their mothers to learn what to expect from a woman, a wife and the mother of his children. Likewise, a daughter will look to Dad to understand what a man is, a husband and a father. Being role models is the most important thing we do as parents. The key is consistency because our children are always observing even if they don't realize it. Parents are being watched and they lead by example. Children will develop what their parents model. So be constantly aware and do your best to set the right example.

If parents model low self-esteem and poor power utilization, it is very likely that will transfer to the children. If parents model good and healthy self-worth, self-esteem and strong and appropriate power utilization, the odds are better that children will do the same.

We all know that there are no such things as perfect parents. Every human being has some flaws, foibles, weaknesses and the like. I am a Certified Family Life Educator by the National Council on Family Relations (Emeritus status). I am qualified to teach parenting. But I am introspective enough to realize that I am not a perfect parent. Therefore, my children need to process the imperfect role model I have been (despite my best efforts) and make their own adjustments in the same way I did with my parents.

Now, I am very much my father's son. We look alike and act alike in many ways. Most of that is quite fine. My dad was a good man, a faithful husband and a hardworking provider. However, he was a product of the Depression. His family had hard struggles during that challenging time. As a result, his primary focus was to provide for his family. He worked about 80 hours a week as the owner of a grocery store, which left very little time for interaction with his two sons. I needed other boys' fathers to assist me in my quest to become an Eagle Scout, etc. I appreciate what my father did for me, but in important ways, he was absent; too busy working as a provider.

We all have our shortcomings and faults. So, children need to take from their parents the best qualities they observe and then sort out the less helpful and do the work/therapy to overcome those negative influences and strive for a healthy ego and self-worth. That's part of the maturation process. It can be difficult work that can take years, depending on the situation, but it is essential to achieve the full embrace of personal power each of us is entitled to.

Speaking of therapy, I have a strong background as a practitioner in the mental health field. I directed the outpatient mental health department at Good Shepherd Hospital in Allentown, Pennsylvania, for more than seven years.

Let's explore Cognitive Therapy, which focuses on the messages we give ourselves. That *self-talk* is called *cognitions*. If we give ourselves positive *cognitions*, we will have a more positive self-esteem. If we continually give ourselves negative *cognitions* (self-talk), we will have a negative self-esteem.

Now, this does not give you permission to be dishonest with yourselves. That's not productive either. But self-talk is healthy when it is framed like this: "Okay, I'm not perfect. But you know, I'm quite okay. I like the person I see when I look in the mirror – faults and all." When we give ourselves affirmations with positive *cognitions*, we enhance our ability to see life more joyful and loving. A steady bombardment of negative *cognitions* will hamper our ability to have joy and love in our lives.

From generation to generation, we pass on good habits and bad habits, good attitudes and troubling attitudes, positive beliefs and confounding beliefs, positive *cognitions* and negative *cognitions*. It takes intentional focus and effort to break the cycle of negative behavior and promote positive behavior. We don't just outgrow those behaviors without putting in the work. They are sometimes even buried in our DNA, which takes a great deal more effort to expunge.

Do not accept the notion that you are not worthy and that you should not assert yourself. That is never in your self-interest. Reject it and stand firm in fair and appropriate ways. To capitulate IS to perpetuate!

Building A Power Portfolio

- In what ways do you diminish your own self-esteem?
  - Where did that come from?
- What kind of home environment were you raised in?
  - What actions can you take to enhance your self-esteem?
  - What challenges your self-esteem?
- In what situations do you feel most vulnerable?
  - What makes it so?
  - How can you address those situations productively?
- What kind of "family of origin" issues do you have that need to be addressed?
  - If you think outside assistance would be beneficial, make a list of places you can go for help and perform your due diligence to find out which is best for your situation.

6. Building Power Confidence

Most of us know the expression, "Learn from our experiences." Or perhaps, "The school of hard knocks." The message is that we learn from events in our lives, and that knowledge helps us in the future. I want to challenge that assumption.

If we were more effective at learning from events, then we wouldn't ever make the same mistakes twice. I know in my life I have some things that I do over and over again that I struggle to master. I suspect we all do.

There is a method to assist us in learning from our experiences. I was exposed to this method at a week-long human relations laboratory presented by the Mid-Atlantic Association for Training and Consulting some years ago. The method has an acronym EIAG (pronounced EE-AG).

"E" = "experience." We have an experience from which we want to learn something that will aid us in our future. It may be an experience that did not go well, and we don't want to make the same mistake again. Or it may be an experience that went very well, and we want to repeat that same success.

"I" = "identify." We identify one particular aspect of that experience that we want to better understand for the future. We select one element within the experience that we believe was pivotal to its failure or success. And we seek a deeper and more thorough understanding of that element.

"A" = "analyze." We want to dive deeply into a specific element in the experience that we have selected to gain a more thorough understanding of all its components and dimensions. This is where the real work is done. We take that element, tear it apart into little pieces and explore each segment to gain a complete understanding of all aspects involved. The greater the analysis, the more fruitful the learning. And this is where we often fail in our daily lives to learn from our experiences. We fail to dissect them and investigate each tiny component.

"G" = "generalize." Once we have thoroughly explored the aspect of the experience that we want to learn more about, then we ask, "What would I do differently the next time?" "Whenever I am in a similar event, how do I want to respond to gain the most positive results?"

The EIAG process steps are:

1. Have an experience from which you want to learn.
2. Identify some segment of that experience that you can improve upon for the future.
3. Analyze that segment thoroughly and in great detail to glean every tidbit from it to feed your learning. The deeper the dive, the richer the reward.
4. Generalize how you want to act the next time you encounter a similar event or situation.

Let me give an example. I am now in my early 70's (yes, I am old!). I no longer have the agility or grace I had in my younger days. Which is to say, I am getting a bit clumsy.

In particular, I notice that when I walk down a flight of stairs, I sometimes catch my heel on the step I am leaving to move to the step below. This causes me to stumble, and I have even fallen once. This is not a good thing, and I don't want to make that a habit. So, I want to EIAG the event.

E = the experience is walking down the steps

I = catching my heel on the step I am leaving and stumbling

A = dissect the event into its parts and discover what I am doing wrong.

G = generalize so I don't do that again.

In my analysis, I discovered that I am not lifting my foot high enough to clear the step and/or am not moving it out far enough.

In further analysis, I learned that it usually happens when I am not focused on going down the steps but am distracted by other environmental factors, or am involved in other thoughts and not being attentive to the task at hand.

I know I am the kind of person who can be easily distracted. This is nothing new. What is new is being older and less agile and adroit. I apparently need to make some compensation for my age in this process. In my younger years, going down a flight of stairs was automatic. In fact, I could scurry down the stairs quite rapidly without incident. Not anymore.

To generalize so I don't continue to stumble and potentially fall, I have come to these conclusions:

1. Stop at the head of the stairs and gain my focus. Be clear that my task at hand is to maneuver down the steps without trouble. Stop thinking about other things and train my attention to this effort.
2. Be aware of the movement of my leg and foot. Am I raising it high enough? Am I moving it forward appropriately – far enough but not too far? Am I placing my foot on the proper location on the next step? And so forth.
3. If I am carrying items, have I secured them in a manner that does not block my view or inhibit my motions? Am I trying to carry too much? Am I being prudent about this effort?

I believe that if I take the time to run through this simple checklist before I embark on my journey down the steps, I will minimize or even eliminate the possibility of future mishaps. That's EIAG!

Let me use another example. Strangely, I am an undefeated collegiate soccer coach who never played soccer outside of high school gym class. Here's how I applied EIAG in that endeavor.

Since we did not get films of our opponents ahead of time, we could not prepare for their unique way of playing the game. Instead, we had to get ourselves in good condition and know how we were going to effectively play the game the way we know how and in a way that fits the skills of the members of our team.

However, halftime was our chance to EIAG. I believe that halftime in an athletic event is one moment coaches really earn their pay.

As my players gathered on the sideline to rest and got some liquid into them so they didn't dehydrate, I sought their opinions about how the game was going. They were the ones on the field. What did they see that I may have missed as their coach? We especially focused on understanding how the opposition was attempting to play the game, and how it matched or disrupted our efforts. Where were the trouble spots, and what could we do about them?

E = the soccer game and our dedication to be victorious

I = some aspect of our opponents' actions that impeded our path to success

A = what were they doing – in as great a detail as possible; what difference was it making; how can we counter or overcome it?

G = compose a plan for the rest of the game that would chart an improved course to our victory

Obviously that method worked, since my teams ended each season undefeated.

EIAG works with much more than manipulating our way down a flight of stairs or obtaining victory in sports.

EIAG is a methodology to authentically learning from our experiences. Yes, it takes time, but it is time well spent to enhance our future endeavors.

This is what I believe the vast majority of us fail to do.

And failing to genuinely learn from our experiences will only cause us to repeat the same mistakes over and over until we finally embrace a better way.

Repeating our mistakes is to squander our power. Why waste our power repeat the same flawed efforts? Why not learn to pause, take an experience, identify what is in that experience that is crucial to its success, analyze that aspect thoroughly and dive deeply into its every aspect so that we can then generalize a more productive path forward?

Manifesting a life that is more satisfying is worthy of some expanded effort. To fail at such a discipline is to capitulate to the faults and failures that inhibit us. That's diminishing our power needlessly.

I hope you will embrace this method and apply it to a wide range of opportunities. Every experience we have is rich with the chance to learn how to engage life more fruitfully.

It can be in our relationships – fertile ground for this enterprise. Why do we get ourselves into trouble in certain places or with certain people? How can we better diagnose the context and discern a better way of engaging? A rich opportunity to EIAG!

At home, at work, in school, at play – wherever, we can enrich our lives by this simple but effective tool.

Building A Power Portfolio

- Pick an experience you would like to better understand.
- Identify one element within that experience that seems pivotal.
- Analyze that element in depth. What about it makes it pivotal?
  - What is each little piece that applies?
  - In what ways do the various pieces fit together or work against each other?
  - What more can we learn?
- Generalize for the future. What can we do differently that will ensure greater success when a similar situation confronts us?
  - What can we learn from this exercise?

7. Managing Power Relationships

One of the most frequent ways we squander our power is **by poor and ineffective conflict management**. We handle the conflict in all the wrong ways and therefore waste our time, energy and power without achieving a desired goal.

So, let's dive into conflict management and see what we can learn. Please note the **Conflict Management Grid** below.

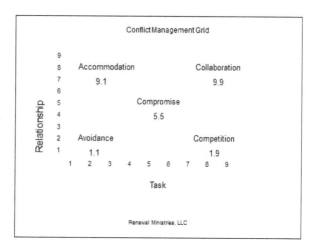

The Grid has two variables. On the left, or vertical scale, we measure the importance of the relationship or cooperation on a scale of 1 to 9. A 1 means the relationship is not very important and we don't want to invest much of our power and energy pursuing it. A 9 means the relationship is very important and we want to ensure its wellbeing and health. So, we will gladly invest a considerable amount of power, energy and cooperation to maintain the relationship.

Across the bottom, or horizontal scale, we measure the task or need to be assertive scale from 1 to 9. A 1 means the task is not at all important and we need not waste our power or energy being assertive. A 9 means the task is terribly important, and we want to heavily invest our power and assertiveness to achieve its success.

Note, there are five options for every conflict:

1. Accommodate
2. Avoid
3. Compromise
4. Compete
5. Collaborate

Every one of those options can be the correct choice sometimes. And every one of those options is can be the incorrect choice sometimes. There are two skills needed to successfully manage conflict:

1. Have all five options in one's conflict management repertoire – which is to say that we are competent and skilled and comfortable using all five of these options at the right time and in the right way. What usually happens is that we have a preferred option that is our default style with which we are most comfortable and proficient. After that, we may have one fallback style with which we are familiar; not as comfortable or proficient, but able to use if necessary. And that is it. Rarely do we have within our conflict management repertoire all five with which we are both skilled and comfortable using. That's our starting point.

2. Know which conflict management option to use when and how. Just being capable of using all five is not enough. We need to appreciate the value of each option in each situation so that we can effectively engage in the conflict appropriately with the

most productive outcome. Remember, power means "getting what I want."

"What I want" will vary in every conflict situation depending on the circumstances. Perhaps I want to achieve a certain goal – like win a race. Or perhaps I want to establish and deepen a more substantial relationship. Or maybe I just want to extract myself from an uncomfortable situation that seems to be going nowhere. Which is to say, much of this is contextual. What is in my best self-interest varies from context to context.

Conflict Management Grid

Okay, let's take a thorough look at each of these five conflict management options to see what works or doesn't work in certain contexts. In the lower left-hand corner is Avoidance. It is labeled 1.1, meaning that the relationship is not important nor is the task. It is not worth any measurable investment of power or effort. Note: this is the lose/lose option. No one wins and nothing gets done.

Proper uses of Avoidance are:

- If the issue is *trivial* and no one really cares about its outcome or the nature of relationships. Why argue over something that is going nowhere?
- There is a *hopeless resolution* – we could go on forever and never come to any agreement – why squander our power in such a useless manner?
- When *cost of the confrontation is too high* – in order to accomplish any degree of success, it will require a higher investment of power and energy than is warranted. It just isn't worth it.
- When *unable to take the stress* – perhaps this event is happening in the midst of a troublesome time or experience and we just do not have the energy to engage and instead need to invest our power in a more productive way.
- When *others can solve it better*. I am neither an accountant nor

a lawyer. When either set of skills is required for the situation, why should I waste my time and power trying to solve something that is clearly out of my range of skills to manage? Delegate the task to those better qualified.

Improper uses of Avoidance are as follows:

- No *real communication*. If you and I are having a conflict and instead of engaging in a constructive way to resolve the conflict, I use my energy and power to avoid you or anything to do with the conflict, then all I do is perpetuate the conflict in an unresolved status. No resolution is possible.
- *Energy is misplaced*. Instead of investing in problem solving, I am taking my energy and using it to stay away, deny or otherwise avoid engagement. I am investing my power in a useless and perhaps even counterproductive manner. I am wasting my power avoiding.
- *Decision made only by default*. Without proper engagement in the conflict, any decisions that get made are made in "cruise control" or default, and they may actually take us off course and into undesirable directions. Poor use of power.
- *Compliance without commitment*. Avoiding each other, we may settle for some kind of off-hand solution to which neither of us are committed. We just want to move on and not face the difficulty of the conflict, which will likely result in an unsatisfactory outcome.

Now we move to the upper left-hand corner, Accommodation. This is labeled 9.1. It is 9 on relationship but only a 1 on task. It is the "you win/I lose" option. There are proper uses and improper uses. The proper uses are:

- When I realize that *I am wrong*. If I am wrong and you are right, I should accommodate to your position and relinquish my position. That demonstrates courtesy, and it maintains a healthy relationship. My willingness to admit my error builds trust to strengthen the relationship and make it more dependable.

- When the *issue is more important to you than it is to me*. If this is something in which you are highly invested and I really don't care, then okay – let's do it your way. This, by the way, is also a *power currency* that will enhance my ability to get what I want in return when I am more invested than you are.
- *Goodwill gesture.* This can simply be a way for me to be a good person and allow you to have what you want this time. It enhances the relationship and shows my respect for you and your position. And it is also a *power currency* I could benefit from later.
- *Build up social credits* (power currencies). If I am more cooperative now, that will increase your ability to trust me and be more open to my suggestions when I am more invested in an outcome.
- *When it is more important to preserve harmony than to achieve the task.* This could be especially early in a relationship as we seek to measure how much we can trust each other or how safe we determine we are with each other. Building a degree of trust and safety will enhance more productive outcomes in the future. For now, let me be open to your ideas so that later you will be more comfortable being open to my suggestions.

Improper uses of Accommodation:

- It renders me with *no influence, reflection or recognition*. If all I do is continually accommodate and give in to everyone else's ideas or requests, I gain nothing and squander my power to get what I want.
- *Deprives others of my contributions.* Perhaps I have a brilliant way of resolving conflict but refuse to share it. Then I squander both my power and the power of others to advance productively.

- *Cost to the user is burdensome.* Why do I never get anything I want? Because I always give in! Come on!
- *Creates an unpredictable emotional climate.* Why does a person always give in? What's going on? Is that person really engaged in the enterprise? Can that person be trusted?
- *Creates a false sense of cooperation.* Does one person really always agree or is this just a phony way of operating? What does that person really think?
- *Builds only a one-sided relationship.* By always giving in, I abandon my side of the relationship which only creates a tension and quandary about my true investment in the effort. And I never get what I want.

Now we move to the center of the Conflict Management Grid – Compromise.

The biggest misconception about Compromise is that people believe this is a solution and that the problem solving is done. "We reached a Compromise, we are finished." That is not necessarily true and a common mistake.

Note that in Compromise we both win some and we both lose some. It is only a moderate way of resolving the disagreement. Neither of us leaves fully satisfied. We merely took a Compromise instead of a full solution.

Compromise is an intermediate level of assertive and cooperative; issues tend to come back. Perhaps that is why we keep fighting over the same things again and again? Maybe we have not invested our full selves in the delicate and demanding work of diving deeply into the issue to ferret out all its components and seek a complete and satisfactory solution that will please both sides? This happens too often in government and explains why so much is never resolved.

Proper uses of Compromise:

- It is too costly to fight, but differences are too great for either side to give in (accommodate). Both sides are deeply invested in their positions to the point that it would be unethical for either side to abandon its position.

- *Opponents of equal power and strong goals.* There is no dominant side that could control the outcome. Both sides are equally dedicated and determined.
- *Time pressure.* When something has to be decided due to all kinds of factors that beg for a solution now!

In other words, when this is THE BEST YOU CAN GET, then it is appropriate to temporarily take the Compromise. But remember it is only temporary.

Improper uses of Compromise:

- *Deflects attention from the merits of the issue.* When Collaboration is demanded but instead, we Compromise, we made a mistake.

Next, we go to the lower right-hand corner of the Conflict Management Grid – Compete. This is labeled 1.9. It is a 1 in relationship – we don't care if you like us or not, we just want to win. And a 9 on task – we value the task as the most important thing and therefore are terribly assertive – perhaps even aggressive. It is the "I win/you lose" option.

Proper uses for Competition:

- In an *emergency* – we don't get to vote if we all want to go outside when the fire alarm sounds. In a dangerous situation, decisions need to be made without regard to relationships.
- *Enforce proper but perhaps unpopular rules.* Sometimes it is done just because that's the way it is done whether we like it or not. Those are the rules.
- The *issue is vital to an organization's or a person's welfare.* Civil Rights are an example. It doesn't matter if we agree to not – it is just fair.
- To *stand up for your rights.* When self-esteem or self-worth is at stake, it is necessary to stand firm and say "No." This is not

debatable.

Improper uses of Competition are:

- *Closing yourself off from the help and input of others.* If I am engaged in competing with you, my focus is defeating you (I win/you lose). I am shutting myself off from your assistance or suggestions. This diminishes my power to find the best solution. You may have discovered a way for both of us to win, but I am too shortsighted and blinded by my own aggression to be open to your input.
- *Close subordinates off from learning.* If my management style is to assert my way (or the highway), then I make no opportunity for subordinates to engage in a mutual process of learning and discovery for the best solutions.
- *Might gain only surface compliance.* Since this has been an aggressive process, those who capitulate to my control will likely do so with resistance and not be eager to fully participate as best they could. They have no OWNERSHIP in the solution, as it was demanded of them without their input. So, what's their investment in the outcome?
- *Creativity of the loser is diminished; goes into defending or counter attacking rather than supporting.* Since this was forced upon them, they may determine that their self-worth and self-esteem have been threatened or at least disregarded and may decide they need to assert themselves in ways that could be counterproductive.

Finally, we come to the upper right-hand corner of the Conflict Management Grid – Collaboration. We label this 9.9. It is a 9 in relationship – maintaining a positive and rewarding relationship for it is seen as a high importance. And it is a 9 in task – the desire to accomplish the task evaluated as equally important to the maintenance of the relationships. Both are of the highest regard. Neither is less important than the other. We call this the win/win option. Both sides come out as winners. There are both high uses of cooperation and assertive action.

Proper uses of Collaboration are:

- *Results in a well-rounded, fair, integrated solution; most important when the stakes are high.* The sense of this being a critical task that is essential to the well-being of the group, family or organization as well as the individuals in it.
- *When high commitment is necessary.* We not only need to collaborate on making the decision, we also need high commitment to complete the decided action.
- *Works through hard feelings and builds trust.* The more we experience a win/win atmosphere, the more we feel safe and eager to participate. Where we are fully valued and appreciated as ourselves and critical parts of the picture and not just pawns in a game the more that we are willing to engage. This also results in a higher degree of follow-through to completion. Win/win is rewarding on many levels.

Improper uses of Collaboration:

- *Makes too much of the trivial* (mountain out of a molehill). When the importance of the task is exaggerated.
- *Avoids personal responsibility.* When one side is clearly wrong, they need to own that and no longer seek to win but rather Accommodate properly and politely to the other side.

There is an obvious outcome to this analysis. If my goal is to "always get what I want," then the only conflict management strategy that makes sense is Collaboration. When I play win/win, I win – and so do you!

There is one critical element in win/win. As I am dedicated to winning – I must also be dedicated to your winning! If all I care about is my winning, that is not Collaboration. That is Competition.

In Collaboration, both sides must be fully and faithfully dedicated to each side coming out of the situation feeling like a winner.

Does that mean that both sides got everything they wanted? Not necessarily. Part of the in-depth process of Collaboration is the open and honest dialogue of what each other **needs** to get in order to feel they won.

I may want it all, but in honesty, if I got 75%, I would be fully satisfied. I may want it all, but I really don't **need** it all. So, what is my threshold for honest satisfaction? This has to be genuine. It can't be "well, this is what I'll take for now." That's not Collaboration. That's Compromise. There is a big difference.

In Collaboration, I sincerely evaluate what I really need to claim success. Note, this is where our long-term self-interests often come into play. Do I really need that much? Can I be quite content with less? How much do I **really** need?

This is where mutuality and congenial dialogue are rewarded. Collaboration is usually not the easy solution. It takes time, open and honest conversation, and a willingness to see it through to the end. It is the most demanding of the five conflict management options, but it is also the most rewarding.

If I always want to win, then Collaboration is my option of choice.

Now, how do we get the "other side" to meet us in Collaboration? If they are not willing to make the same commitment to problem solving, what can I do to invite them into this level of engagement?

Let's start with those in Accommodation or Avoidance. They are all invested in relationship and not in task. How do we invite them into a more dedicated stance regarding the task?

Unfortunately, we live in a consumerist culture. The main concerns of our current culture can be summarized with these statements:

- Why should I?
- What's in it for me?
- What am I going to get out of it?
- What's it going to cost me?

I find this terribly sad but also accurate. Therefore, we must engage them where they are. We must invite them into considering their direct benefits of achieving the task. What will they get out of it? At the end, how much better off will they be for the investment of the time and energy (and power)? What outcomes will be there for them that are desirable? Why is it worth their while?

That's the movement on the task scale.

The movement on the relationship scale (from compete to collaborate) looks different.

Many people compete out of a blind self-interest that is not in keeping with their long-term self-interests. In a consumerist, short-sighted fashion, they go for the quick gain rather than an enduring outcome.

Often this is manufactured by negative self-talk (cognitions) that assert a compromised self-esteem and instead inserts a mentality of victory as the key to self-worth. If someone is not strong in the relationship endeavor, they may abandon that effort and seek the individualistic, consumerist path instead. Winning is all they know how to pursue.

Taking the risk to invest in relationships may have proven painful in the past and therefore they are reluctant to move in that direction. Relationships are always a gamble. Some are successful and rewarding. Many are not. It is completely understandable why anyone might be shy when asked to invest in a new, unproven relationship. Makes sense.

Therefore, the primary challenge in getting someone to move from Compete to Collaborate is to build trust. We need to provide evidence they can trust us. Sometimes, this may call for the use of Accommodation in the beginning of a relationship as a means to build social credits that can grow into a trusting relationship. BE CAREFUL not to establish a one-sided relationship with expectations of always capitulating. That is not desired. But some initial willingness to Accommodate may be fruitful. "What can I do for you? How can I assist you?"

Building trust depends on another key factor – safety. People can only trust when they feel safe. "How do I know you won't betray or abandon me? How do I know I won't get hurt?" That's a critical challenge. Demonstrating our dedication to their welfare as well as our own is the task at hand. It will take patience and endurance. But without it, we will not get to Collaboration.

Collaboration is built on trust. Trust is built on safety.

To summarize what we have proposed so far in this chapter, since most people have only one preferred or default conflict management strategy with which they are comfortable and believe works for them, they therefore lack the full range of options and so diminish their power and chance for success.

To comfortably acquire all five conflict management options is to first understand them in depth and then practice, practice, practice.

Become familiar with our desired conflict management style and why we think it works for us – when often it does not get us to Collaboration dependably. Analyze the self-talk (cognitions) that convince us to use a particular preferred conflict management style when it may not be all that effective. And explore new, more beneficial self-talk that will move us in a positive direction. "Why do I do it that way? What is a better way for me to operate? How can I get there?"

Reach out to others who are likely in the same quest. Therapy can be helpful here as well.

I truly believe we are bestowed with all the power we will ever need. We are just so bad at using it.

Let me venture one more strong example of conflicting management styles. I want to juxtapose John Wayne over Mahatma Gandhi. If you are not very familiar with Gandhi, please do some research. Gandhi led a non-violent movement to free India from British rule – actually a much harder task than it might seem.

By John Wayne I don't mean the real person, but the one we know from the movies. John Wayne's conflict management style is competition, pure and simple. Wayne is the strong, independent, don't-need-anyone's-help tough guy who can defeat any foe. And so, he does.

Gandhi, on the other hand, won his struggle – not alone, but by launching a movement of active, non-violent resistance. Gandhi stood strong against fierce oppression and injustice. But he never used violence.

In the end, Gandhi wanted the British to be friends. You don't make friends using the John Wayne approach. You make people your friends by showing them their errors and caring for them in the process. Do not shame or embarrass your foe. Treat them the way you would want to be treated, but do not participate in their injustice.

Gandhi was a master at moving the British from Compete to Collaborate. I think we need to learn from him.

Further, reflecting on our codependence aspects, Wayne is a classic Quadrant II: The hero who rescues the poor victims who are too incompetent to rescue themselves. "I alone can save you!" is the Wayne attitude. So, he muscles his way through, saves the damsel in distress and wins the day like no one else can.

On the other hand, Gandhi is Quadrant I. The power of active resistance is the power of the truth, and it seeks a win/win solution without the use of violence. We want to convert our opponents, not hurt them. We want to unite our efforts and function together for the greater good. That's the Gandhi method. Far healthier.

Not with bullets or guns, but with the strength of truth and a refusal to capitulate to injustice, Gandhi taught us the true meaning of power.

Building A Power Portfolio

- What is your primary or default style of conflict management?
- What is your fallback option in conflict management?
- How can you become more proficient in all five conflict management options?
  - What do you need to do?
  - Who can help you do that?
  - Who will hold you accountable in the effort?

- Where do you fall on the Wayne-Gandhi spectrum?
  - What do you know about Gandhi?
  - What can you do to better understand non-violence and make it a part of your repertoire?

8. How Conflict Affects the Bottom Line

I'm going to begin this chapter by discussing types of conflict. My source for this is the book *Intervening in a Church Fight: A Manual for Internal Consultants* by George Parsons (Alban Institute). While Parsons is writing for a church audience, the wisdom of the book fits across the culture.

I am taking Parsons' material and giving it my own interpretation.

Let's start with one of the most complex of conflicts, a values conflict. The classic example relevant for the time of this writing is the progressives versus the conservatives. We are in the midst of a "tribal warfare" that pits these two factions against each other in what seems to be an impossible skirmish.

However, values conflicts can be resolved, especially when both sides desire to stay together (like in a family unit).

Values Conflict:

- Provide training to increase tolerance of differences. This does not happen without some intervention. So, engage whatever resources are needed and do the work of building mutual respect and tolerance.
- Use fair and rational decision-making. This needs to be a thoughtful process where emotions are kept in check.
- Provide opportunity to talk across lines, to share positions, interests, values, feelings and feedback. Ask each side to share what others see as its negative or problematic aspects. "What could be seen as troubling in our position?"
- Find behaviors or tasks that can be done together, even if for opposite reasons. An example is the abortion debate. Pro-life people and pro-choice people can work together to avoid unwanted pregnancies.

- Keep the conflict on the issues, not on personalities. Deal with facts more than opinions.

In a group or family situation, another difficult conflict appears if one or more members are incompetent. How do you fire a relative?
  Incompetence Conflict:

- Where it makes sense, face the reality of removal from the position. Hard to do in a family unit. Requires thorough analysis and appropriate action. It helps if a "file" has been built over time identifying specific problematic behaviors – when, where, what, with what consequence, etc.
- Strictly follow due process that is fair, using feedback, training, support and re-evaluation.
- Make the decision to stay or go based solely on established policy.

Next is a conflict over goals and methods. Where do we want to go and how are we going to get there?
  Conflict of Goals or Methods: Follow a Problem-Solving Process

- Clearly define the problem and/or desired outcome. When we are done, what did we want to accomplish? Remember Stephen Covey: "The main thing is to keep the main thing the main thing."
- Carefully and thoroughly collect data. Do this well but be careful not to fall into "analysis paralysis."
- Generate a range of alternatives. Avoid binary thinking as much as possible. When we have only two choices, the odds of picking the wrong one or not successfully completing the desired outcome are fairly high. Simply adding one more option to move away from binary thinking, even if the added option is not practical, opens our minds to a different kind of processing that generally yields better results.
- Test and examine the alternatives. I tend to be a bit of an

idealist – "This is supposed to work." So, it is wise to do some "reality testing." Yes, in an optimal circumstance, that is supposed to work. But are these optimal circumstances? Do we need to factor in the real elements facing us? An example: I have an axiom, "You are as sick as your secrets." The more secrets an individual or group has, the more pathology. So, ideally, we ought to expose and eliminate all our secrets. However, that demands a very emotionally healthy environment for that to be successful. So, better not give that a try in a less than fully healthy situation.

- Chose an alternative. Once all the possibilities have been faithfully evaluated, select the one that has the best chance of meeting the overall goals. Then make a commitment to it.
- Plan the action. Dive into the who, what, when, where and how in a step-by-step fashion to map out the course of agreed-upon action.
- Actually perform the steps as carefully planned. Expect that all will not go perfectly and build in an ongoing evaluation process for corrective action along the way.
- Evaluate the outcome. Did we end up where we wanted? How did the process unfold? What problems did we unexpectedly encounter? Why didn't we anticipate those problems? What can we learn from this endeavor? Remember EIAG? What would we do differently the next time? Where do we go from here?

Let's now venture into interpersonal difficulties: When folks have a hard time getting along with each other. Note: We will visit this again later when we look at personality types.

Interpersonal Difficulties: Unmet needs for inclusion, feeling powerless, desiring more affection or sensing lack of recognition. Many interpersonal conflicts will have special dynamics.

- Team-building activities designed to facilitate the issues of inclusion, proper levels of affection and recognition as well as power dynamics. These are best when led by a qualified professional. Therapy is a form of this intervention.

- Skill-building activities such as listening, mutuality, power analysis, etc.
- Interpersonal conflict training to include the preceding chapters on power utilization and conflict management.
- Problem-solving process (see above).

Another familiar conflict is the lack of success, inability to achieve, frustration and blaming.

Lack of Success, Inability to Achieve, Frustration, Blaming

- Clear assessment

  - o What are the causes of decline or failure? Honesty and openness are critical elements in this process.
  - o What are the resources needed and how do we make them available for success? Pride sometimes comes into play. Folks hate to admit they need help, so make things like coaching and mentoring a standard part of the culture.
  - o Establish manageable and realistic goals. Are we trying to do too much too quickly?
  - o When necessary, admit demise or failure and bring to a healthy closure. Not everything succeeds. Often, we learn more from our failures than our successes. Remember Thomas Edison. Make room for a grieving process.
- Engage a problem-solving model (see above).

There is also the conflict of being bored, apathetic, frightened or in denial. These are often intentionally hidden. "We don't have any problems here."

To solve conflicts characterized by being Bored, Apathetic, Frightened and/or In Denial, follow this process:

- Supportive listening. Create a safe place for folks to be open

and honest without judgment.
- Review of past experiences. What went wrong? What went right? How can we learn from this? What will we do differently the next time? EIAG.
- Pull learnings from past conflicts. When this happened before, how did we resolve it? If it never got fully resolved, what residue do we want to avoid this time? What do we do now?
- Set appropriate goals that will challenge the bored and apathetic but not aggravate the frustrated. Reach those in denial with reality testing.
  - Goals that are:
    - Behavioral
    - Achievable
    - Specific (what, when, where, how)
    - Personal (who)

One of the most painful conflicts is the breach of the system's (personal, family, organization) trust, especially when perpetrated by a revered leader. This could be theft, sexual or any other kind of boundary violation.

Breach of Trust resolution process:

- Due process must be meticulously followed for everyone. Stick to established procedures
  - Do not re-victimize the victim
  - Arrange treatment for the perpetrator
  - Care for every individual involved, directly or indirectly
  - Healing for the system

Next is a structural conflict where the system itself needs repair. Things are not functioning in a good order. Note: A system can be an individual (how are we getting along with ourselves), a family, a work environment or an organization.

Structural Conflict:

- Establish clear and adequate channels of communication throughout the system. What kind of self-talk (cognitions) am I giving myself? How effectively and appropriately are we communicating within the system?
- Establish clear lines of authority that do not conflict with each other – a clear "chain of command." Personally, will reason win over emotions?
- Create a fair and reasonable method for making decisions such as voting versus consensus. Maintain consistency in that methodology so individuals are comfortable in the process. Variations can occur but must happen with mutual understanding and agreement.
- See that power is fairly and reasonably distributed within the system. Note: It is more powerful to empower than to hoard power.
- Establish clear role expectations. What are the limits and expectations? Are these clearly understood and documented? How much power inhabits each position?
- Make clear all the system's norms, folkways, customs, etc. so newcomers can quickly fit in and feel comfortable and safe.

Five Levels of Conflict

That completes this review of types of conflict.

We move now to levels of conflict based on the work of Speed Leas of the Alban Institute. I will use his work with my own adaptations.

There are essentially five levels of conflict. Ideally, we will keep all our conflicts at Level I, where stress and anxiety are at a minimum and confidence for an easy and amicable resolution are high.

Level I: A problem to be solved. Both parties fully believe they can easily resolve this conflict themselves in a quick fashion with virtually no animosity or distress.

Characteristics of a Level I Conflict:

- A real conflict, not just a misunderstanding

- Actual differences exist
  - Different
    - Goals
    - Values
    - Needs
    - Action plans
    - Information
  - Low level discomfort in the situation
  - Anger is short-lived and quickly controlled
  - Objective = to fix the problem and move on
    - Use rational methods to determine what is wrong
    - Problem-oriented, not personal-oriented
    - Optimistic about resolution
  - Language
    - Clear
    - Specific
    - Here and now
    - "Adult," not judgmental or childish
    - Not blaming
  - Movement to resolution is fairly easy

Level II: Disagreement. The levels of distress and anxiety are a bit higher, moderate, but not to any extreme.
  Characteristics:

- Objective = self-protection, to not get hurt or taken advantage of, "looking out for myself"
- Rise of shrewdness and calculations
  - Networking
  - Strategizing
- Language: From specific to general
  - "Some people" rather than names
- Not hostile, just cautious

- Limited sharing of what one knows
- Trust issues arise

Level III: Contest. Now we move from protecting ourselves to wanting to win, to defeat the "other."
Characteristics:

- Win/Lose dynamics
- Objectives = from self-protection to winning
- Often more than one problem exists yielding factions or coalitions in tension with each other
  - Issues and causes
  - Taking sides
  - Power or control issues
- Use of distortion makes matters worse
  - Perceptual distortions = a serious problem – each side sees it only their way
  - Magnification = sees oneself more benevolent than one actually is, and the other side more evil than it actually is
  - Dichotomization = dividing everything and everybody into a binary view
    - Us versus them
    - Right versus wrong
    - Stay versus leave
    - Loss of shades of gray
  - Over-generalization = one specific behavior is evidence to document larger categories; i.e. untrustworthy, out of control and/or pernicious (insidious, fatal), quality arises, i.e. "you always" "you never" "everybody"
  - Assumption = delude self, can do mind reading of opponent's intentions and motives, i.e. "you're trying to get me to make things worse"
  - Resistance to peace overtures
    - Looking for each other's vulnerabilities

- Personal attacks are endemic at this level.

Level IV: Fight or Flight

- From wanting to win to wanting to hurt the other
  ◦ The other will never change
  ◦ Only option is to get rid of them
- Good of the subgroup over the good of the total group
  ◦ We are right; we have the moral authority to punish opponents
- Factions solidify, clear lines of division, strong leaders emerge, subgroup's cohesiveness is valued over survival of the total organization/system
- Language = ideologies, principles more than issues (truth, rights), ends justify the means
- Brings out primitive survival response on both sides (fight or flight); no middle ground is perceived
- Cold, detached, unforgiving, self-righteous
- Use outsiders only to help defeat or expel the others

Level V: Intractable Situations
   Characteristics:

- Unmanageable; conflict run amok
- Each party out to destroy the others; they are wicked and harmful to society
- We are part of the eternal cause; fighting for universal principles
- Must fight; dare not stop – costs of stopping too high to society, truth, righteousness, etc.
- Costs of defeating the others is less then costs of submission to their evil

Examples of Level V conflicts are nuclear war, radical cults and other expressions of total intolerance.

From Leas' explanations, the goal is to keep all our conflicts at a Level I, where the stress and anxiety levels are low and confidence for resolution is high.

Reflecting on the Conflict Management Grid, we know that to achieve that kind of healthy and successful collaboration requires an atmosphere that is trusting and safe. The more we can establish comfortable relations, the better our chance to manage conflict amicably.

The more we emphasize our differences via racism, political opinions and such, the more we minimize our power to achieve successful conflict resolutions.

Investing the effort to build trusting and safe relations that empower each other, and expressing mutual respect is the most effective way to "get what we want" in keeping with our long-term self-interests.

Building A Power Portfolio

- What *type* of conflict do you often encounter? Identify its characteristics.
- What *level* of conflict do you generally encounter? Define its components.
- How can you help establish an environment that keeps conflicts at a Level I?
    - What specific steps can be taken immediately?
    - What are some long-term interventions that may be needed?
- What kind of internal conflicts do you experience?
    - How does the material in this chapter help you address those conflicts?

9. Smart Power Investing

One way we diminish our power is to squander it on trying to solve problems that cannot be solved. We call this polarity management. My main source for this is the book *Polarity Management: Identifying and Managing Unsolvable Problems* by Barry Johnson (HDR Press, 1992). What I am presenting here is my own interpretation of this issue with a look to power utilization.

Polarity is a condition when two sides of an issue have equal value and validity. Both sides are respected and make legitimate offerings to the issue at hand. An example that fits our current political situation these days is conservative versus progressive. Conservatives have much to contribute to the welfare of our nation as do progressives. We waste our power and energy trying to decide one or the other.

Polarity management places these two "opposites" in a grid to analyze each other's strengths (positives) and drawbacks (negatives). The grid would look something like this:

Capitalism—positives	Socialism—positives
• Inspires competition • Rewards hard work • Rewards those who get ahead (the "lead dogs")	• Inspires collaboration • Rewards teamwork • Rewards the success of the community over the individual
Capitalism—negatives	**Socialism—negatives**
• Discourages collaboration • Economic Darwinism • Leaves the less skilled or those with less opportunity behind	• Stifles individual initiative • Inspires mediocrity (I "get" no matter how hard I work or don't) • Denies the "human nature" to want to be the best individual of them all

Likely, where one stands on each of these sides will bias how one reads my analysis. I have tried to be neutral so we all can get the picture of how polarity management works.

A key element is the respect for and valuing the input from both sides.

One fundamental aspect of good polarity management is sensitive to the horizontal line that runs across the middle of the grid and separates positive from negative. A good polarity manager will be alert to that threshold. As soon as our actions or opinions cross into the negative quadrant on the grid, we need to move to the positive quadrant on the other side.

So, on the conservative side, when we notice that we are being too tight with resources (i.e. funding, etc.), stifling innovation or smothering creativity –we need to move to the positive side of progressive. In the same way, when we move to the negative side of progressive and are abandoning the tried and true needlessly, or fiscally irresponsible and chaotic, we need to go to the positive side of the conservative.

Warning: When we are beginning to cross from positive to negative on any side, the correct response is the diagonal move. To simply dive deeper into the negative side in hopes of creating a resolution will only make things worse. So, if we become too conservative and things are becoming stale and in want of new energy, infusing more conservatism will only make things worse. Likewise, if we are too progressive and are no longer fiscally responsible, then providing a greater dose of progressiveness will not resolve the situation. The middle horizontal line is the line of acute awareness that it is time to move to the diagonal positive quadrant.

Let's give it another shot using some of the dynamics of the Myers-Briggs Type Indicator (MBTI). In the MBTI, everyone is either an Introvert or an Extrovert. Both have merit.

Introvert–positives	Extrovert–positives
• Reflective, think before acts • Processes internally • Does not speak until sure of what to say	• Engaged with others • Expressive • Energetic
Introvert–negatives	**Extrovert–negatives**
• Isolated • Appears aloof • Too introspective, too slow to respond	• Can act before thinking • Too overbearing • Can't relax and be reflective

Clearly, being Introvert or Extrovert is the right way to go. It is just how we prefer to live. Both sides have equal merit and the positive sides of both contribute genuinely.

Let's try a fun one with regard to parenting. One debate in raising children is if we should take major vacations while the children are young to give them exposure to other cultures, ideas, etc., or save that money instead for their college educations.

Let's lay that out as a polarity.

Grand Family Vacations–positives	Save Money for College–positives
• Provide high-quality experiences for the children • Inspire their intellects and expand their perspectives • Build some lovely family memories	• The money will be there when the time comes • Avoids burdening the children with college debt • Teaches fiscal responsibility
Grand Family Vacations–negatives	**Save Money for College–negatives**
• Breaks the bank with no money left for college • Sets "unrealistic" expectations for the rest of their lives • Spoils the children	• They are children only once and deserve opportunities for fun • Deprives the children of mind-expanding experiences • Deprives the family of some exciting memories

The same goes here. Both sides have some legitimate merit. Where do we draw the line? Well, the line is literally drawn in the middle of the grid. Breaking the bank for an experience the family really cannot afford is not productive. Nor is being too fiscally cautious and in doing so depriving the children of some learning experiences that will be advantageous and productive for family memories.

Polarity management is literally balancing two opposing but equally valuable positions. One side alone is not entirely correct. Correctness is found in a healthy balance of the two.

Let's risk one more – Capitalism versus Socialism. Sure, let's give it a go!

Capitalism–positives	Socialism–positives
• Inspires competition • Rewards hard work • Rewards those who get ahead (the "lead dogs")	• Inspires collaboration • Rewards teamwork • Rewards the success of the community over the individual
Capitalism–negatives	**Socialism–negatives**
• Discourages collaboration • Economic Darwinism • Leaves the less skilled or those with less opportunity behind	• Stifles individual initiative • Inspires mediocrity (I "get" no matter how hard I work or don't) • Denies the "human nature" to want to be the best individual of them all

Ideally, we would take the best of both positive sides and build a culture that benefits from both opinions. It inspires innovation but for the sake of the community and not the individual alone. It rewards collaboration without some recognition of individual accomplishments. It leaves no one behind without ignoring the attitude that hard work deserves rewards. The problem in our "tribal" society is that one faction has made an enemy of the other (approaching a Level IV conflict) and now only sees how it can defeat the other, viewing it as evil. The more we linger in that approach, the more we deprive the goodness that can come from a more balanced approach. Take the best of both sides, weave it together and make it work.

I hope you are getting the nature of polarity management. If we are struggling to resolve a problem that just never seems to go away, perhaps it isn't a problem to be solved at all. Most likely, it is a polarity to be managed just like the examples above.

Wasting our time and power on such fruitless endeavors is not productive. Instead, let us invest our power into diving deep into the polarities, clearly identifying the middle horizontal line and keeping a watchful eye for when we need to move to the opposite diagonal. That's power utilization!

Building A Power Portfolio

- Where do you find polarities in your daily life? Define the two sides.
- Practice working a polarity. Map out the positives and negatives of each side.
- How can this discipline help at home, work or other places?
- What can you do to be an advocate for polarity management in situations you encounter?

10. Power Theory Investments

In this chapter, I want to explore Systems Theory and Transactional Analysis. Each of these holds great potential for investing our power.

My understanding of a system is the interdependent functioning of the component parts. For example, the human body is composed of a skeletal system, a muscular system, a nervous system, a digestive system and all the rest. None of those systems is independent; to function effectively there needs to be a wholesome balance and interdependence among all those systems.

Another way to conceive of systems theory is a mobile hanging from the ceiling. A good mobile has a delicate balance among all its parts. They hang in a precise way to allow for the effect desired. Remove one of the parts and the whole mobile is thrown out of balance. Increase or decrease the impact (i.e. weight) of one of the parts and again the balance is disturbed and needs to be reconfigured.

Systems theory is the appreciation of that delicate and interdependent balance. Families are a system. Just exactly how do Mom, Dan, Junior and Sis get along with each other? Is it a healthy balance that allows each to function as Quadrant I entities? Or does one member of the family dominate and demand the subservience of the others to maintain a balance that is not healthy? What happens if one member of the family changes, leaves or otherwise moderates its behaviors and attitudes within the family? Again, a rebalancing is demanded, or the system will not function.

From a power analysis, one cannot change the other parts of the mobile, the system. One can only change oneself.

From the example in the chapter on codependence (Mom, Dad, Junior, Sis) where Dad is a drunk; Mom, Junior and Sis cannot change Dad. But they can change the way they interact with Dad and with each other. If Mom, Junior and Sis collectively insist that Dad get sober or get out, that is a change they can manage within themselves. Dad then must decide to get sober or get out (to rebalance the system).

So, the power utilization learning from this aspect of systems theory is that when we are in a system (home, work, school, etc.) where things do not function in a healthy way, trying to change any other aspect of the system other than ourselves is a waste of power. It just doesn't work. The only part of the system we can change is ourselves. Understanding that changing how we function within the system will require the rest of the system to rebalance itself.

Note: Depending on what we do, the system could change for the worse or the better. Even if we move from Quadrant IV to Quadrant I it does not guarantee that the system will respond positively. In fact, the system may well rebel against the fact that our change now requires that rebalance of the rest of the system. Even if the system is a dysfunctional system, to its components, that dysfunction is familiar. They all know how to behave within the dysfunction. Asking them to find new attitudes and behaviors is asking them to change. And the change is what they may well resist even though the change you made for yourself is the correct one for you. We cannot determine how others should respond.

Change theory tells us that all change requires stress. When we move from one balance of the system, no matter how dysfunctional, to a new rebalance of the system, it means that each of the component parts has to let go of the familiar and venture into the unknown until a new rebalance is determined. That rebalance will not be automatic or simple. It will require considerable work for each of the component parts to do their own self-searching and analysis and seek new behaviors and attitudes to adopt. That will take time, trial and error practice and all the rest.

To go from the familiar into the unfamiliar is to venture into the unknown which is stressful. Even a positive change like getting married requires each spouse to reassess their place in the relationship. Once each person was single. Now each is married. What does that mean? What does that demand? Where is this going? How will it end?

So please recognize that all change is stressful, yet movement from any other Quadrant to Quadrant I is productive for the individual and needs to be reinforced with strength and stamina. Systems are like mobiles: Change one part and all the others are impacted.

Another important aspect of systems theory is how a healthy system deals with the impact of a toxic.

Using the human body – when it is healthy (has a healthy immune system). When a toxin enters the human body, the immune system within the body forms antibodies that surround the toxin and minimizes its impact until the toxin can be removed from the system. The ability to form those antibodies quickly and effectively is a key activity of the immune system. When the immune system is weak, it cannot perform effectively.

As with the human body, so it is with any other system. Say with a family, when a toxin, say Dad's drinking, enters the family, then the rest of the family needs to dramatically form an antibody response to that toxin and neutralize it until it can be removed from the family.

It doesn't have to be addictive substances. A toxin can be any unhealthy attitude, such as racism or Antisemitism. Or it can be Quadrant II, III or IV behaviors or attitudes. To maintain a healthy family system, all such toxins must be recognized for what they are, neutralized and removed.

And what is true for a family system is also true for a school, an organization, a church, at work – wherever. Healthy systems will not tolerate the presence of a toxin within the system. A healthy system will immediately recognize its presence and effectively neutralize and remove the toxin.

Good power utilization is the immediate ability to identify and label a toxin, play a vital role in neutralizing it and effectively drive it out of the system.

Being unable to identify a toxin when it enters the system is to diminish one's power and thereby being forced to dwell within an unhealthy system.

It is terribly difficult to remain healthy oneself within an unhealthy system. Which is to say, it is terribly difficult to remain healthy within an unhealthy family – an unhealthy school – an unhealthy workplace or organization.

And since most systems are not perfectly healthy, then an ongoing task for any system is to be perpetually vigilant for toxins. Our culture is full of them. The biggest one has already been identified – consumerism – What's in it for me? Why should I? What am I going to get out of it? What's it going to cost me?

It is a challenge on a daily basis to remain so constantly alert to toxins and then to individually respond and hope that the rest of the system will also recognize the toxin and appropriately respond.

One way to know there is a toxin within a system is to identify the anxiety.

Anxiety within a system is like a red flag that something is out of balance. A toxin that has intruded itself within the system needs to be identified and expelled.

This begins with anxieties within us. We squander our ability to be powerful when we fail to identify and own our anxieties. What spooks us? Why does it spook us? Is that reaction an appropriate reaction? Some things are legitimately spooky and ought to spook us – if they don't, then something else is wrong.

But when our reaction is debilitating rather than wholesome, we need to dive deeply into that, identify its component parts, understand a better way to function and implant that new behavior or attitude for the future (EIAG).

A key way to deal with anxiety is to have a *non-anxious presence*. When we are in the midst of an anxious situation, within ourselves, within our families, our work, our church, wherever, to be able to have the strength and the power to remain calm infuses the situation with a wholesome element that can have a positive impact on the situation.

Having a *non-anxious presence* does not usually come automatically. It takes practice. It takes wisdom. It takes an ability to assess the situation, understand its components, evaluate the stress and anxiety and stand firm and steady when addressing the problem (EIAG).

The power of someone with a *non-anxious presence* is large. It is like a calm oasis in the midst of a desert of stress and can bring the water of hope and optimism that a positive result is possible. To be present in confidence and a steadiness that holds firm and does not fall apart when others are going up the walls puts one in a power position for the sake of the total situation. It is not a tool to use to manipulate the event. The desire to manipulate maliciously seldom comes from a *non-anxious presence*. The desire to manipulate comes from Quadrant II. A *non-anxious presence* comes from Quadrant I – a win/win position.

A *non-anxious presence* comes from an ability to be "centered" – to be able to take a deep breath, to be self-aware and to be steady ready to engage productively despite all the craziness around us. Again, that comes from practice and a confidence that this works – because it does.

Remember: Systems are like a mobile hanging from the ceiling. As long as all the parts are in a proper and healthy balance, all is fine. When the system gets out of balance due to a toxic or whatever, then the only thing we can change is ourselves and then play our part reasonably to construct a healthy new system for the whole.

Now let me move into Transactional Analysis. The key book here is *I'm Okay, You're Okay* by Thomas Harris.

Transactional Analysis (TA) is really a reworking of Freudian psychology.

Freud came up with the Superego, the Ego and the Id.

Harris renames these the Parent, Adult and Child. Transactional Analysis is a wonderful way to figure out why some interactions don't work well.

It looks like this:

Person One	Person Two
Parent	Parent
Adult	Adult
Child	Child

In TA, as the two people interact, as long as the lines of the interaction are parallel, the interaction will go okay. For example, if two well differentiated adults are interacting with each other, that will go well.

However, if one person is trying to be a healthy, differentiated adult, seeking to interact with another healthy differentiated adult, and the other is acting like a child seeking to connect with a parent, the interaction will not go well.

But if one is acting like a parent and another like a child, it could go well. The parent may be seeking a child to parent. And the child may be seeking a parent for comfort and security. It goes well – even if both are actually adults.

My wife and I like to act silly from time to time – being childish. As long as both of us have the same childish expectations of each other, it goes well. But if one of us is tired of being childish and wants adult interaction but the other remains childish, we need to resolve that.

I used the term "differentiated" – that means a well-identified self who is at a proper stage of maturation and equipped to behave appropriately. That usually means a Quadrant I person. Persons outside of Quadrant I are generally not well-differentiated.

In terms of power utilization, ideally we will all be Quadrant I persons, well-differentiated and mature and able to shift from Parent, Adult and Child in a manner appropriate to the situation. Adult is not correct all the time. Even well-differentiated Adults need to play from time to time, embrace their playful Child and have fun.

Even well-differentiated Adults may need to get strict from time to time and lay down the rules like a disciplining Parent – OR act like a comforting Parent to someone in a distressed Child mood.

Each is correct in one way or another. Like good conflict management, we need to be competent and comfortable with all three – Parent, Adult, Child.

Being well-differentiated – having a healthy self-image, self-esteem and self-worth that does not ignore our weaknesses and faults – is what makes embracing all the options possible.

To compromise our self-differentiation is to diminish our power and render us less effective at getting what we want in keeping with our long-term self-interests.

Building A Power Portfolio

- How healthy or unhealthy is the system in which you live? Define.
- What personal changes do you need to make to be a healthy component in that system?
  - Who will help you make those changes?
  - Who will hold you accountable?
- How will you manage if the rest of the system rebels against your changes?
  - What do you need to resist their efforts to make you less healthy again?
- In Transactional Analysis, from what position (Parent, Adult, Child) do you usually function?
  - How mature and appropriate is your Adult?
  - What would others say about that? Ask some.

11. Understanding Your Value

Shakespeare wrote in <u>Hamlet</u>: *"This above all: to thine own self be true, and it must follow, as the night the day, thou canst not be false to any (person)."*

To thine own self be true... How profound.

I want to propose in this chapter that the better we know ourselves, the more likely we are to get what we want and the more powerful we are.

The opposite is also true: The less we know ourselves, the less likely we are to get what we want. If we don't even know who we are, how can we know what we want? Or are our longings compatible with who we truly are? Perhaps we are chasing after all the wrong things – much like pursuing our short-term self-interests rather than our long-term self-interests.

It is a much-needed adventure to increasingly understand just who we are.

To assist us in better knowing ourselves – at least on a psychological level – I am going to use the Myers-Briggs Type Indicator (MBTI), a product of Consulting Psychologists Press, Palo Alto, CA. I need to give credit to my mentor with the MBTI, Otto Kroeger.

The MBTI is an instrument that measures preferences – and only preferences. It does not measure intellect, abilities or anything else. However, if we are going to attempt to gain what we really want, then knowing our preferences is a valuable asset in that venture.

An exercise to demonstrate this – please write your signature with your **other hand**. What was that like? Difficult, confusing, needed more concentration, felt foolish? That's what happens when we do not function in the areas of our preferences. If I practiced my signature with my other hand, I could become quite proficient with it. It would take a great deal of effort over some period of time, but I could master my signature with my other hand. I am capable.

In the MBTI we do not measure ability, only preferences.

The MBTI measures on four different scales. Everyone is either an Extrovert (E) or an Introvert (I), a Sensing (S) or an Intuitive (N) [we use the N because we used the I for introvert], a Thinking (T) or a Feeling (F), and a Judging (J) or a Perceiving (P).

Let me flesh those out.

Extrovert shares these characteristics: desire for action, energy, externalized, expansive, outgoing, verbal, people oriented, socially oriented, open about personal issues, tend to be verbose and redundant, "after the horse is out of the barn", say it then decide if you mean it, etc.

Introvert shares these characteristics: ideas, concepts, verbally reserved, fore thinker (think it before you say it), energy internalized, less disclosing of personal issues, meditative, reflective, articulate, etc.

Sensing shares these characteristics: concrete, facts and figures, five senses, literal, details, practical, present oriented (here and now), sequential, digital, tactile, prefer tradition (the tried and true), etc.

Intuitive shares these characteristics: other worldly (there and then), dreamer, visionary, inventive, abstract, theoretical, imaginative, idealistic, pictures and symbols, etc.

Thinker shares these characteristics: non-personal, objective values, analytical, questioning, seeking clarity, objective, linear, logical, rational, "makes sense", etc.

Feeler shares these characteristics: personal, subjective values, sentimental, agreeing, harmonizing, subjective, circular, emotional, resist conflict, etc.

Judger shares these characteristics: right versus wrong, structured, ordered, disciplined, methodical, critical, organized, systematic, planning, "bottom line", neat, decisive, categorizing, strategizing, "closing", regimented, purposeful, exacting, compulsive, etc.

Perceiver shares these characteristics: open ended, carefree, easy, unstructured, flowing, adapting, changing, free, spontaneous, curious, flexible, etc.

Thus, everyone is a composition of four letters. For example, I am an ENFP (extrovert, intuitive, feeling, perceiving). My least preferred is ISTJ (introvert, sensing, thinking, judging).

To ascertain your "personality type" – your four letters – I highly recommend *Please Understand Me* by David Keirsey and Marilyn Bates. The version of the MBTI in that book is shorter and all one normally needs. If you want to go deeper in the MBTI, you will need to consult a clinical psychologist.

Please note, there is also the dynamic of the strength or weakness of our preferences. For instance, I am a very strong ENFP – not likely to vary at all and very comfortable with my preferences and very predictable. If, on the other hand, someone has weak (low score) preferences, it means they are not as decisive in their preferences and the good part is that they are more flexible.

Strong scores have the advantage of comfort and are determined but predictable. Lower scores have the advantage of flexibility and able to do one or the other but have less comfort with one or the other and are not predictable – those with lower scores never know which one they will choose and when.

Also, our preferences can vary with different situations. At work we might prefer to operate one way, and at home an entirely different way.

However, overall, it is helpful to know our preferences to better and more deeply know "who we are" – so we can be true to ourselves.

To help you figure out what your preferences are, let me share some "tests."

To determine E versus I – define an ideal vacation. And E will want lots of going and doing. And I will want quiet, peaceful, meditative and so forth.

To determine S versus N – look at an object and define it. An S will be very objective (size, shape, smell, etc.) while an N will be creative and subjective (what could be done with that object, more creative).

To determine T versus F – describe a good teacher. A T will want a well-prepared teacher, knowledgeable, able to transmit information well, etc. An F will want a teacher who cares about the students, is compassionate, individually focused, tender and/or caring.

To determine J versus P – try to make a decision. The J will be brief, direct, bottom-line and concise. The P will take forever and continually expand the options.

Hopefully this will help you determine your four letters.

Another advantage of the book *Please Understand Me* is that it breaks down the 16 possible personality types to just four **temperaments**. A temperament uses only two of the letters.

Keirsy and Bates discovered that if one is an N then they are either an NF (intuitive feeling) or an NT (intuitive thinking). In the same way, if one is an S then they are either SJ (sensing judging) or SP (sensing perceiving).

Let's explore those.

As an ENFP, I am therefore an NF. The characteristics of an NF are: people oriented, catalysts (bringing people together), arch idealists, avoid conflict, interpersonal, authority is in the person, persuasive, "need affirmation", always seeking personal identity (who am I?), Achilles heel is guilt, etc. NFs are only 12% of the population.

The characteristics of an NT are: loves conceptualization, quest is "why" (why are we doing this instead of that?), strive to be highly competent, anti-authority (need to prove your expertise), visionary, big planners, always their own worst critic, the "better idea" person, etc. They compose only 12% of the population.

The characteristics of an SJ are: structure, scheduled, ordered, loves procedures, rules and regulations, quest = what needs to be done, do not tolerate disorder, like to belong because in belonging one gets the "rules of the game," Achilles heel is disarray, "don't fix what isn't broken," very much into tradition, etc. They are 38 to 40 % of the population, but 80% of the military.

The characteristics of an SP are very present-oriented (here and now), quest is "when" (when can we get started?), seek action, very misunderstood and under-valued, skilled craftsmen, Achilles heel = inaction (just wait), etc. They are 34-36% of the population.

NFs and SJs can get along with each other. NFs seek identity and belonging that gets them the identity of that group (I'm one of them). SJs seek belonging because being a member provides the rules and regulations of the group.

NTs and SPs can get along with each other. NTs seek competence, and action provides them the chance to be competent. SPs seek action, they can't bear to just sit around and the more competent they are the better chance they have for action.

NFs and NTs may not "play well with each other." NFs are very people oriented and tend to find the NTs cold and aloof. The NTs are into doing things a better way and may offend people with their rejection of the status quo or the way the NF has been doing things.

SJs can have a hard time tolerating SPs. SJs seek tradition, the tried and true and an orderly and well-thought-through procedure, while SPs just want to get going and figure it out along the way. SPs can't stand the rigidity of the SJs and their "analysis paralysis" – SPs just want to get into action and not spend so much time on policies and procedures.

So my message for this chapter is that the better we know ourselves, the greater chance we have to "be true to ourselves" and thus be more effective in pursuing our long-term self-interests. "How can I know what I *really* want if I don't even know very well who I am?"

I believe the MBTI is a superb tool for getting to know ourselves better and deeper. "Why do I gravitate toward certain people more than others and certain environments and activities?" "Why do certain people just annoy me more than others?" "Why don't I find certain activities very satisfying?"

Again, the MBTI only measures preferences, not abilities. I was a top math student in high school. I could have been a good and competent accountant. But sitting at a desk all day crunching numbers would be torture, and the person I am wants to be around people and desires to be out and about. That's the kind of thing I am arguing for. Knowing that I am a strong ENFP or NF can guide me toward a more satisfying career, group of friends and rewarding activities. Not knowing these preferences is to diminish my power, my chance to get what will be satisfying and rewarding – what I **really** want – my long-term self-interest. Why deal with frustrating pursuits when with the help of instruments like the MBTI I can better know myself and be more true to myself?

Clearly, the MBTI is not the only instrument that can assist in this better understanding of the self. There are others. I have used others and been trained in others, but I strongly perfer the MBTI.

Building A Power Portfolio

- What is your personality type (your four letters)?
    - How do you feel about that?
    - Are you comfortable with who you are?
- What is your temperament (your two letters)?
    - How accurately does that define you?
    - If not, what should be different?
- With which other of the four temperaments do you get along best?
    - Get along worst?
    - Why do you think that is so?
- How can the MBTI be a tool to help your power utilization?

12. Promoting Power Collaboration Growth

Let's begin by reviewing some of the critical aspects we've identified so far.

My definition of "power" is "the ability to get what I want."

That leads us to the appreciation of long-term versus short-term self-interests. We need to understand our long-term self-interests and not be seduced by short-term temptations.

"Group" refers to any setting that involves two or more people. It could certainly be one's family – even if the nuclear family consists of only two spouses – that is a group setting.

Group entails a work setting, social setting, other organizations – especially volunteer organizations.

Wherever two or more people are together, that is the "group" addressed in this chapter.

We need to keep in focus the paradox that to horde power is to diminish our ability to get what we want. To empower enhances our ability to get what we want.

In this chapter, we combine the Co-dependence Chart and Quadrant I plus the conflict management material and the desire for the win/win solution. We don't need to be subservient to anyone, nor do we need to sacrifice our wants because of the pressure from others. The win/win strategy firmly states that we assert our needs (spend our personal power) while valuing the needs of others and assisting them in meeting those legitimate needs. Collaboration (more than one person adding to a power account) is the best way to operate and build value faster. If that fails after appropriate efforts, then other conflict options can be considered.

However, in this chapter, the focus is on the dynamics that will assist us in achieving collaboration more successfully, thus building our personal power quickly.

To that end I am citing two contemporary books. The first is *Switch: How to Change Things When Change Is Hard* by Chip and Dan Heath (Broadway Books, 2010).

In *Switch*, the authors point out that there are three key components to bringing about change in a group setting. They consist of the "rider," the "elephant" and the "path."

The rider symbolizes the intellectual or rational aspect of change. What makes sense? What is the logical thing to do? Here, we look at the "why" of the change.

Note that the rider is much smaller than the elephant. So even with the best logic and reason, if the elephant believes otherwise, the rider is not going to get where he or she wants to go.

Let's begin by focusing on the rider. *Switch* recommends three things to consider.

The first is to "follow the bright spots." *Switch* illustrates this with a situation where a person was disturbed about work that needed to be done. There is immobilization in that person's distress. When asked what happened when work got done more easily, the person reflected that relaxation seemed to facilitate a more productive outcome. So, the "bright spot" was to learn to not get anxious but to just relax and get to the task and things get done.

The "bright spots" are those moments or elements that make things work: when goals were achieved and when production happened. Taking time to reflect on those positive elements can guide us how to act in the future. Very similar to the EIAG process reflectively.

There is a school of psychotherapy called Solutions-Focused Therapy. The process goes like this: A patient comes in anxious and worried about something. The therapist takes the time to gently listen, understand and build rapport. At the proper moment, the therapist reflects that the patient seems to be functioning reasonably well right now. What is currently working for the patient that allows the patient to operate now? Focusing on the patient's strengths rather than their anxiety helps the patient apply the strengths and skills the patient already has in an effort to relieve the anxiety and properly address the new context. The solution comes from what the patient already knows how to do rather than asking the patient to try a new approach. Solutions-Focused Therapy – the bright spots that already exist in the patient's life.

The second strategy *Switch* gives to help us persuade the "rider" is to "script the critical moves." Don't think "big picture," but rather more specific and workable steps that can be addressed now. "What often looks like resistance is often a lack of clarity."

An illustration was that West Virginia University was trying to persuade individuals to have a healthier diet. Milk is a key part of children's diet, yet milk is also a key source of saturated fats. So, by merely suggesting that children drink 2% milk provided a simple and accessible solution. Script the critical move. Not a big picture, but a neat way to address the problem.

The third way to assist the "rider" to make a change is to "point to the destination." Change is easier when you know where you're going and why it's worth the effort.

To illustrate this, *Switch* presents the story of Crystal Jones, who taught a first-grade reading class. She excited and motivated her class by saying that at the end of the year they would all be "third graders" in their reading skills. Certainly, it is cooler to be a third grader than a first grader. "Yeah, let's go for it. Let's be third graders by the end of the school year."

Motivating a group to achieve a goal that is exciting for them is far easier than just telling them what to do. Point to a destination that is attractive and achievable and that makes sense. We can do this!

That's how we address the "rider." An even bigger challenge is to motivate the "elephant."

The "elephant" represents the emotional side of the change. As a rule, even reasonable people resist change. As presented in change theory, to go from one way of doing things that is comfortable and familiar to a new way of doing things that is not familiar and will necessitate some stress and discomfort is daunting. How do we overcome that?

Switch presents three ways of dealing with the "elephant."

First is to "find the feeling." Knowing something is the right thing to do is not enough to cause change. Making people *feel* something is right and desirable facilitates the change.

To illustrate this, *Switch* presents a case of a company that required employees to wear work gloves. There were a wide variety of work gloves for the type of work to be done. An intern discovered that there were 424 kinds of work gloves used in their factories. Further, these were being bought by a number of different suppliers. The same glove bought from one supplier cost $5, but from a different supplier cost $17! So, the student collected a sample of all the 424 gloves and placed them on a table with the price tag labeled on each. As the company executives viewed the display, they did not realize the wide range of gloves they were buying and the great variety of cost. Clearly, the executives recognized the problem and were motivated to make a change. Not only could they "see" the problem, but it touched them as to the craziness of the situation. They "found the feeling" to make a change.

The second way to address the "elephant" is to "shrink the change," to reduce it in size and scope so that it isn't so oppressive. Break down the change until it no longer spooks the participants.

The illustration here is from Marla Cilley. She came up with the "5-Minute Room Rescue." The problem was the resistance by some to launch into doing tasks like cleaning a messy room. We are great at making marvelous excuses to procrastinate work that needs to be done.

Instead, Cilley suggested merely taking a kitchen timer and setting it for 5 minutes. For that brief time, apply oneself to the task less desired. At the end of 5 minutes, one can stop and accept the reward of getting something done. In truth, once in gear and moving, at the end of 5 minutes, one just might want to continue until the task is fully completed. But initially, the commitment was for only 5 minutes. It's a neat way to "shrink the change" until it is less threatening.

The third way to approach the "elephant" – the emotional side of making the change – is to "grow the people." This is to cultivate a sense of identity and instill the growth mindset.

There is the expression, "the only constant is change." When a group embraces a concept and makes it less threatening, change is far easier to adopt.

To illustrate this concept, *Switch* points to a company called Brasilata that made tin cans. The standard for the industry was that a can needed to survive a drop of about 4 feet without damage to the contents if it were to contain dangerous or flammable substances. Most manufacturers simply made the cans thicker with more metal. This increased the cost. But Brasilata took a lesson from the automotive business with collapsible bumpers and made their cans able to take a minor dent without threatening the contents – a much more cost-effective method.

Brasilata had established the value of adaptation and change in their company and thus made finding a new way easier to discover and apply. "Grow the people" is an environmental approach that must permeate from top down and from bottom up. It must be in the DNA of a group. It is who they are and how they operate.

Now we move to the "path." How do we make the destination desirable?

Once again, *Switch* presents three approaches.

The first is to "tweak the environment." When the situation changes, the behavior changes. So – change the situation.

A psychotherapeutic approach known as Behavioral Therapy uses this technique. Simply by getting people to do the new behavior even though it is awkward and stressful is a quicker way to gain compliance than to sit around and wait for agreement. Psychologically, if we are doing something, then by the mere fact that we are doing it will quickly convince us that it is okay. We adapt faster to the new behavior by launching into it rather than squabbling over it.

Switch illustrates this with the principle, "tweaking the environment is about making the right behavior a little bit easier and the wrong behavior a little bit harder." An example is moving to a new phone system that is less complex and easier to use.

The second way to address the "path" is to build habits. When behavior is habitual, it's free all its own without the pressure of the "rider." Look for ways to encourage new habits that embrace the desired change.

An illustration here is in a recovery institution for patients with knee or hip replacements. They introduced the "habit" of writing down an "action trigger" on paper such as "going for a walk this week." They discovered dramatic results. "On average, action-trigger patients were bathing themselves without assistance in 3 weeks, compared to the 7 weeks for other patients. Action-trigger patients were standing up at 3.5 weeks rather than 7.7 weeks. In just more than 1 month, the action-trigger patients were getting in and out of a car on their own versus the 2.5 months for others."

To "build habits" most effectively requires the collaborative process that produces "ownership" of the individuals that need to embrace the change. What would make habit building work for them? How can they be included in the process as the patients were noted above? Empowerment is a catalyst for the successful movement.

The third way *Switch* points to adapting the "path" is to "rally the herd." Behavior is contagious. Once a number of people are doing it, others will follow. This helps to spread the new behavior.

Switch illustrated it this way. In Tanzania, there is extreme poverty in many areas. As a result, wealthy men could manipulate young women into compromised situations with temptations. How can they address this?

There is a word is Swahili, *Fataki*, which translates as "explosive" or "fireworks." By labeling these wealthy men and their temptations as *Fataki* and broadcasting that regularly through the media, the word caught on and helped to label a problem so that it is better understood and resisted. They "rallied the herd" through a media blitz that expressed the challenge in an easy to appreciate way, and that caught on quickly and effectively.

Switch is a book I highly recommend for all to dive deeper into these methods to bring change to groups when change is hard.

The next book I want to suggest is *Canoeing the Mountains* by Tod Bolsinger (IVP Books, 2015).

In quick summary, Lewis and Clark made their journey up the Missouri River with the expectation that once they reached its end there would be a mountain, and over that mountain would be another river that would take them to the Pacific Ocean. Simply venture up one river, cross one mountain, and then make one's way down another river to the ocean. A challenge, but manageable.

However, when they got to the end of the Missouri River – yes, there was a mountain. BUT there was another mountain, and another mountain and a whole range of mountains.

The problem was that Lewis and Clark were river navigators. They were not mountaineers. They did not have the skills and experience or equipment to make their way over mountain after mountain. They had journeyed beyond their range of expertise.

This dynamic is often true in group changes where the group needs to go beyond its current skill set. They've never gone there before, never done that before, never been like that before. It requires something else.

In my discussion of the Myers-Briggs Type Indicator, there are also the concepts of stretch and bridge. To stretch is to learn new skills and abilities. To bridge is to connect with someone who has the skills and abilities we don't.

In the case of Lewis and Clark, they did not have the skills or experience needed to traverse mountains. They were already well into their journey with no time to go back and acquire the needed expertise. Instead, they needed to bridge to someone else who could guide them. In comes Sacagawea, a Lemhi Shoshone woman, with the skills and experience so necessary for the success of the expedition.

Lewis and Clark had to first admit that they were now out of their range of expertise. They didn't have the knowledge and training for the current context. They didn't know what to do or how to do it.

They had to admit they needed help. Step one in making progress is admitting we need help.

Step two is finding the help. In this case, it was a Native American woman. I suspect it was an "ego challenge" for two men of that time to accept the leadership of a woman, a Native American nonetheless! So, dealing with one's pride and accepting the help of others can be an issue. Help may come in surprising ways. We need to be open to all kinds of possibilities. Who knows where the help will come from?

Next, Lewis and Clark had to abandon their canoes. The canoe for them was essential. That was their stock and trade. They were river navigators. They were nothing without their canoes. How could they abandon them?

But canoes are just in the way when one is traversing a mountain. The time came for them to embrace new "technology" for the new challenge.

Which begs us to ask, what kind of "canoes" are we clinging to in our lives, or in the life of our group? What do we now call essential that needs to be discarded in order to move the group forward? How can we effectively identify those canoes and find the courage to abandon them? Who will lead us? How will we get there?

There is a great deal to learn from the adventure of Lewis and Clark. I strongly urge reading *Canoeing the Mountains* for its insights and wisdom.

Utilizing power in the context of a group requires attention to the "rider," the "elephant" and the "path." What will it take to address the needs of each of those in a productive way that moves the group ahead in a collaborative fashion that renders a win/win solution for all?

When will we know that we left the river and now need to cross over the mountains? Will we be ready to accept that we no longer have the expertise within the group to manage the situation? Will we be open to outside help? How will we find that help? Will we accept new leadership?

And dare we abandon canoes that we cherish but are no longer useful and may even inhibit our progress?

These are some of the concerns that need to be addressed in the context of power in a group.

Building A Power Portfolio

- What is in the way of "the rider" in your group for making the needed change?
  - How can that be addressed?
- What is in the way of "the elephant" in your group for making the needed change?
  - How can that be addressed?
- What is in the way of "the path" in your group for making the needed change?
  - How can that be addressed?
- Is your group ready to admit it may not have all the skills and expertise it needs to move forward?
  - Is the group ready to abandon some beloved canoes that just aren't what the group currently needs?

13. Balancing Your Power Portfolio

Stress management is the topic of my doctoral thesis, *Helping People Understand and Manage Their Stress* (Drew University, 1982). This thesis is a key source for this chapter.

Let's first get an understanding of stress.

"Stress is a contributing factor in 90 percent of all diseases, according to Dr. Kenneth Greenspan, director for the Center for Stress Related Disorders at New York's Presbyterian Hospital." As many as half of all visits to the doctor's office are stress related. (Burlington Free Press)

One of the most respected experts in the field of stress is Hans Selye, a medical researcher in Montreal. He states that stress is "essentially the rate of wear and tear in the body." And Selye defines stress as "the nonspecific response of the body to any demand." (The Stress of Life, McGraw-Hill)

Hippocrates, the father of medicine, told his disciples that disease is not only suffering (pathos), but also toil (ponos), that is, the fight of the body to restore itself toward normal. Nature has its own healing force. (The Stress of Life)

The great French physiologist, Claude Bernard, "taught that one of the most characteristic features of all living beings is their ability to maintain the constancy of their internal milieu, despite changes in the surroundings." (The Stress of Life)

Walter B. Cannon, famous Harvard physiologist, said that this power to maintain constancy in living beings is called *homeostasis* (from the Greek *homoios*, meaning like or similar; and *stasis*, meaning position or standing), the ability to remain the same, or static. (The Stress of Life)

Apparently, one does not just suffer from a disease, but we

actually have an internal struggle to re-establish a homeostatic balance biologically as a result. (Stress of Life)

What happens during stress is that chemical alarm signals are sent out by the directly stressed tissues via the nervous system and thereafter to the endocrine glands. The appropriate hormones are produced to combat wear and tear in the body. However, other hormones produced as a result of diet, heredity and nervous reactions, and tissue memories of previous exposures to stress can throw the normal benevolent process off course, thus resulting in diseases of adaptation, or stress diseases. (Stress of Life)

Stress comes in two forms: 1. Harmful or threatening stress called "distress," and 2. Helpful or desired stress called "eustress." Most of our conversation around stress deals with distress. We fail to take into account the impact of eustress.

An event that is perceived to be stressful, one way or the other, is called a "stressor." The body knows no difference between a distress or a eustress. The body just knows that a stressor happened, and it needs to react.

An example of eustress is when the person you love agrees to marry you. Truly it is a moment of great delight. But the body only knows that something big has happened and it needs to react.

When the body is impacted by a stressor, the hormonal system goes into an action we call "arousal." The body leaves homeostasis and goes into fight, flight or freeze. When the stressor is no longer present, the body is supposed to return to homeostasis. This whole process is directed by the autonomic nervous system (sympathetic into arousal; parasympathetic back to homeostasis). A healthy autonomic nervous system handles this without a hitch. An unhealthy autonomic nervous system usually moves into arousal but has trouble getting back to homeostasis. Thus, we get high blood pressure, etc.

Symptoms related to stress disorders as identified by Selye include: general irritability, hyper-excitation or depression, pounding of the heart, high blood pressure, dryness of the throat and mouth, impulsive behavior, emotional instability, overpowering urge to cry or run or hide, inability to concentrate, flight of thoughts and general disorientation, feelings of unreality, weakness, or dizziness, predilection to fatigue, loss of the *joie de vivre*, floating anxiety, afraid although we do not know exactly what we are afraid of, emotional tension and alertness, feeling of being *keyed up*, trembling, nervous ticks, tendency to be easily startled by small sounds, etc., high-pitched, nervous laughter, stuttering and other speech difficulties, bruxism or grinding of the teeth, insomnia, hypermobility/ hyperkinesia, increased need to be in motion, sweating, frequent need to urinate, diarrhea, indigestion, queasiness in the stomach, migraine headaches, premenstrual tension or missed menstrual cycles, pain in the neck or lower back, loss of or excessive appetite, increased smoking, increased use of legally prescribed drugs such as tranquilizers or amphetamines, alcohol or drug addiction, nightmares, neurotic behaviors, psychosis, and/or accident proneness. (Stress of Life)

With such an extended list, it almost seems as though everyone can find something in there about themselves. Which is, perhaps, the point?

One of the best books on stress is *The American Way of Life Need Not Be Hazardous to Your Life* by John Farquhar (W.W. Norton & Co.)

And while much of this language is about the body, we also know from a wide range of studies that it is not merely a physical issue. By "body" in this sense, we really mean **body, mind and spirit**.

We humans are more than just our physical bodies. In fact, another great book on the topic of stress is *Mind as Healer, Mind as Slayer* by Kenneth Pelletier (Dell). The mind and the spirit play equal roles in the management of stress.

It is like a tripod – three legs. A tripod with three healthy legs can stand in any terrain – rugged or smooth.

Our challenge in this chapter is to understand how to keep all three legs of our stress-management tripod healthy so we can effectively use our autonomic nervous system to move into arousal quickly and then return fully and appropriately to homeostasis. I like to call this *maintaining balance*. A healthy system maintains a good balance in the key aspects of life, and thus enables a strong and effective autonomic nervous system. To live life out of balance is to give away our power to do solid stress management and therefore compromise our health – body, mind and spirit.

So, let's launch into maintaining balance. I like to break this down into three major categories – Nurture, Advocacy and Wholeness.

NURTURE

1. Lifelong Student: The more we stimulate our minds, the healthier we keep our mental capacities. To let our minds go stagnant is to welcome dementia and the like. A stimulated mind is a sound mind. It is a kind of mental health that keeps us sharp and intellectually agile. To go academically dormant is to invite a deterioration of our reasoning and problem-solving abilities. To continually learn is to "feed" our intellects and nurture them with new ideas and information. It is food for the brain. To allow our minds to be "starved" is to weaken our ability to address mental challenges and thus diminish our power.

2. Support Groups: Humans are social animals. We are meant to be in groups. As early as the cave people, humans organized into "tribes" for mutual support and safety. Even so today. However, our current "tribalism" can be negative as in one political party against another; as in "us" versus "them." That is the opposite of what I am proposing here. *Support groups* refer to those intentional gatherings of people who make a commitment to be there for each other and provide a significant level of mutual support. This can be a formal gathering specifically designed for this purpose (like AA) OR it can be an informal collection of good friends who enjoy spending time with each other and commit to assist each other in tough times. Such groups require dedicated times to be together, to build a healthy rapport and trust level so that it is safe to be open with each other at appropriate levels and

content. Just a group of friends may not be enough. It needs to be a group of friends who have grown into this way of being for each other in safe and trusting ways. Here's an example: In one faith fellowship, a group of widows organized what was called the "Widow's Wagon." These ladies sat together in worship and went to lunch together afterward. When a new woman was widowed, the group reached out to welcome her into their fellowship. They were there for each other in a host of ways. It was even fun relating to this proud group who turned being widows into a warm and supportive sorority.

3. Therapy: Very few of us are not a bit off-balance emotionally from time to time. I directed the outpatient mental health department at a hospital for more than seven years, and I have a pretty good idea of the general mental health of the total population. A big problem is the stigma given to mental illness. To admit that we are "seeing a therapist" too often is taken as a sign of weakness or insufficiency. That is far from the truth. Weakness is failing to admit the need for outside help. We all go through times of emotional distress that appropriately can be better managed with professional help. It is wrong to think we can always go it on our own. Nonsense. In every life, some tragedy or loss appears that sets us back. To regain balance, we need the careful attention of a qualified professional. And we may even need some psychotropic medicine. The chemistry in our brains can get out of balance and the use of some assistance to reestablish that chemical balance only makes sense for a time. Therapy is not failure. Therapy is the wisdom to know that something is not working and to get the help we need.

4. Spiritual Health: I want to delve into this a lot deeper in a following chapter, but for now, leave it to say that if, indeed, we are mind, body and **spirit**, then we need to be equally attentive to that aspect of ourselves as we are to our physical and mental health.

5. Leisure Time: I strongly believe that no one should work more

than fifty hours per week on average. I recognize that some professions may require extensive work weeks now and then – like an accountant during tax season – but that needs to be the exception rather than the rule. Selye developed a principle called the General Adaptive Syndrome (or GAS...sorry, that's what it is, for short). The General Adaptive Syndrome states that we can only function in arousal for so long. We may think that arousal is just the "new normal" for our lives and that we are managing just fine, we have adapted, but that is not true. Extensive persistence in arousal is exhausting and will take its toll. We cannot remain in arousal for too long. Likewise, our failure to fully and completely return to homeostasis and thus only partially move out of arousal has the same effect. The ability to relax, to let go, to be in a state of leisure on a regular and dependable time is necessary for healthy balance. What works for you is up to you to determine. I have enjoyed sailing. I like reading books. You need to find what relaxes you and dependably spend time on that.

6. Friendships: I already talked about support groups. A support group is a more intense relationship than a mere friendship. Friends are those with whom we can just spend time with and enjoy with no big commitments. It is important to make friendships outside of our work relationships. It is extremely important never to think of our clients as our friends. There is something called "dual relationships." By that, I mean that having the same person as a client and as a friend can cause confusion. Am I acting now to this person as a client, which has its own dynamics, or am I now acting as a friend with an entirely different set of dynamics, rules and norms? Getting those confused can bring about an unnecessary conflict for you and the other person. Be "friendly" with your clients, but understand they are not your friends. They are your clients – and that's enough. When you seek to spend time with friends, do NOT include your clients of any kind. Friends are just that – friends. Know the difference!

7. Confidence in One's Calling: I like to think of our professions as our callings. What am I meant to do professionally? To faithfully discern what I am truly constituted to be and do with my work life is a gift. We should all enjoy and find meaning and satisfaction in what we do. Just to show up and earn a paycheck can be draining. Forty hours a week that we do not look forward to takes a lot out of us. But if we have found occupations that fulfill us and empower us, then we have it right. I also firmly believe that we ought to have fun at work. If work has no fun in it, then we may be in the wrong occupation. Work also ought to awake a passion within. "What am I passionate about? How can that passion be reflected in my vocation?" Confidence in what we do for a living makes a world of difference. Give it a try.

ADVOCACY

We each need to be advocates for ourselves. This is being assertive (not aggressive) as discussed earlier. We need to stand up for ourselves and chart out a path that leads to a well-balanced life.

Set Goals: What do we want out of life? How are we going to get it? No one but you can chart that course and be faithful to it. We need to claim the power over our own courses in life and be intentional about that. If all we are doing is drifting through life and letting other external forces determine our outcomes, we are majorly giving our power away! Do NOT be victims of circumstances. Be victorious. And where possible, take charge to control as many circumstances as you can in your life. Most importantly, be in control of how you respond to whatever comes your way. None of us need to be victims. Remember Viktor Frankl in the concentration camp. No one can take our dignity and our self-worth unless we give it to them. Chart your own course. Be the masters of your own lives. Be proud of the person you see in the mirror.

Control Your Own Calendar: What I find exhausting is when someone tells me that they have no time. Can't do that, I'm too busy. Really? Whose fault is that? Who let their calendar get out of control? That does not need to happen. We can grab ahold of our calendars and reserve time for leisure, recreation, spiritual renewal, family enrichment and all the rest. Don't go around bemoaning that you have no time. Get ahold of your life and manage it effectively (like your bank account) to produce a healthy balance for mind, body and spirit.

Clarify Your Job Description: In our occupations, do we really know the dimensions of our jobs? What exactly is expected of us? Is it a reasonable set of expectations, or is our work getting out of control? We have a key part to play in that. Again, be victors, not victims. Be assertive. Speak up. Take a stand. Negotiate a reasonable job description that is appropriate for that position. Don't be bullied into something that can't be accomplished. And if your place of employment isn't amenable to a reasonable job description, it just may be time to find a new job. Unfair treatment at work is not healthy; it is abusive. And to continue in an abusive environment is certainly not exercising one's power in a healthy way. Like yourself enough to set reasonable limits at work. Do a good job, but don't allow anyone to take advantage of you. We need to like ourselves enough to say "no."

Set Healthy Boundaries: By "boundaries" I mean physical, emotional and spiritual. A boundary is our comfort zone. While I like to hug people, I do have a sense of how close I want to get to whom. I'm not eager to hug a total stranger – nor do I think a total stranger is eager to be hugged by me. I enjoy physical closeness with my family and dear friends. That works. But there are reasonable limits with clients and others. And just because I feel like a hug doesn't mean the other person feels the same. Maintaining healthy boundaries also means respecting other people's comfort zones, too. We have emotional comfort zones in the same way. There are some topics that are just not appropriate in every time and every place. Knowing how to approach a conversation in the right way is to both respect our emotional boundaries and the emotional boundaries of others. Spiritually, each faith system (religion, denomination, etc.) has its ways. Maintaining a healthy spiritual balance is to stay within the bounds of our own faith system while honoring and respecting the boundaries of another's faith system. Just because we don't understand where they are coming from is no cause for disrespect.

Seek Adequate Compensation: We all deserve fair pay for a fair day's work. If we are in a job where that is not true, why are we in that job? And if it seems to be "the best job we can get," let's do something about that. What do we need to do to be able to get a better job? Let's take control and not be victims. I fully appreciate that in some difficult circumstances this is a lot easier to say than to do. But are we being honest with ourselves or just capitulating? Have we given up on ourselves? If so, we have squandered our power big time! We don't need to be victims. We can change our circumstances by applying ourselves in direct ways. Yes, it may require the help of others and some real dedication, but it's time to stop playing the victim role.

WHOLENESS

Now we get into some real stuff that is a different kind of challenge.

Exercise: The facts are clear – use it or lose it! Our bodies need physical stimulation to remain healthy. To not exercise it is to give our power away. It is to minimize our wellbeing and compromise our wellness. It is to not only abandon ourselves, it is also to go all the way to harm ourselves. As I mentioned in systems therapy – when a toxin enters a system, the system needs to be healthy enough to negate that toxin, expel it from the system and remain strong. Exercise is a key part of keeping our autonomic nervous system effective and healthy. There is no getting around that. While I cannot dictate the right exercise regime for you, there are experts who can. Find the help you need and get in shape. To fail to do so is to majorly abandon your power. (Note: Please contact your physician before attempting any exercise program.)

Nutrition: It is said that "you are what you eat." That is literally true. Our bodies are constantly remaking themselves. Old cells die and are expelled from the body. New cells need to be made to take their place. We make those new cells from the food we eat. Thus, "you are what you eat." If we eat junk, our bodies have no choice but to be made of junk. If we eat proper and nutritious diets, our bodies are made of the proper stuff to keep us healthy and maintain a strong autonomic nervous system. It's just that simple. In our culture, a healthy diet is a challenge. We have been seduced to like things sweet and salty. That's been done to us. We need to take charge, exercise our power to choose appropriate foods and eat properly. It's our body. No one can do it for us.

Avoid Addictions: This must seem obvious. But there are all kinds of addictions. People get addicted to gambling. People get addicted to pornography. And of course, people get addicted to alcohol and drugs. The key is to value the person we see in the mirror. How much do you love that person? Do you love that person enough to keep sober in every way? If not, then let's go back to the section on therapy. We need help. If we fail to get that help, we are throwing our power away. If we get the help, we can be free from all addictions. We are using our power in a productive way. Why not?

Relaxation: This is much like claiming leisure time, but I want to go a bit further. In working in the mental health field, I discovered that many people do not have hobbies – things they do just to relax and have fun. Hobbies, when they are not obsessions, can be a vital part of good time management and relaxation. Find what works for you. There are such things as recreational therapists – I kid you not. They will be glad to assess you and help you find what will work for you. Find that hobby and enjoy. Relax!

Meditation: This is different than relaxation. Meditation is active. Relaxation can often be passive, as in taking a nap. Meditation has been scientifically documented as a key factor in being able to respond to a stressor and then better able to return to homeostasis when the stressor is gone. Meditation is active in that it involves a certain kind of activity. We call it "centering." Normally, our minds focus on rehearsing past events in trying to better understand and improve on them. Or our minds focus on upcoming events so that we are prepared. All too seldom, we are purely in the here and now. Being solely in the here and now requires some training and practice. The general prescription is to adopt a mantra, a word or phrase to concentrate on which helps create a sense of being centered. A trained spiritual director or meditation expert can assist in finding a mantra – or you can just pick one on your own. I chose my own. Let me share with you two illustrations of the power of meditation. The first one is a case of the hiccups I had just before an important meeting. I knew I could not go into the meeting with the hiccups. Yet everything I tried to get rid of them failed; drinking water, holding my breath, etc. Finally, I decided to try my meditation. I stood perfectly still, practiced deep breathing and repeated my mantra in my head. Immediately, the hiccups went away.

An even more profound example is when I needed to have a biopsy on a muscle in my left shoulder. Unfortunately, the biopsy had to be done without anesthesia. Yes, I was cut open with a scalpel and then had a piece of my muscle tissue cut out with scissors, all without anesthesia because it would contaminate the muscle sample. The pain was excruciating. One a scale of 1 to 10, the pain level was a 12! How did I manage? I started deep breathing and I meditated and went into a mild experience of being somewhere else. I distanced myself from the pain and endured reasonably well. So well that the physician who was performing the procedure said that I was one of the bravest people he had ever met. I do not hold to my bravery. I do hold to the reward of being able to meditate. Meditation takes us out of the worries and woes of the day, and we go instead to a state of deep relaxation and centering. It is a means of a profound experience of letting go and being open to the inner musings of one's mind and soul. Just being.

Marital Care: Marriages don't just thrive on their own momentum. A healthy marriage, like anything else, requires some "exercise." People grow and evolve over the years. They change. And if two people in a marriage haven't kept in touch with each other, they can grow in different directions. The differences can enrich a marriage or doom it; it all depends on how it is managed. Marriage therapy is not a sign of failure. If one needs physical therapy, one goes to a physical therapist. If one's marriage is becoming dysfunctional, then by all means, get to a marriage therapist. To fail to do so is to squander one's power. In addition, when one decides to get married in the first place, find a professional who will do premarital counseling. I am a trained premarital counselor, and I can tell you that a skilled premarital therapist can identify the problems that might arise in that marriage ahead of time and help the couple build in whatever mechanisms they may need to keep the marriage strong and healthy. To avoid the premarital counseling just because we aren't "into it" is to, again, squander one's power to have a healthy and rewarding marriage. Makes no sense. Keep communicating with each other. Be open and honest with each other. And never stop "dating" each other. Don't take the romance for granted.

Family Care: Raising a family is a challenge – don't let anyone kid you. It takes a great deal of effort. I like to kid that I have found irrefutable proof for the existence of God. That any parent in the entire course of human history has survived having teenagers proves there is a God! Being family does not come automatically. Children don't come with a manual. It takes a ton of tender loving care to make it all work. And I strongly advise parents to realize they don't have all the answers. In many occasions, they don't even know the questions. Our culture is evolving so fast that sometimes the children need to educate the parents. How do you operate the remote control? And remember: To hoard power is to diminish power. To empower is to gain a greater ability to get what we want. So parents, be sure to empower your children. And children, be sure to empower you parents!

Family-of-Origin Healing: I am a certified family life educator (emeritus status). I am fully qualified to teach parenting. But I can assure you that I have not been a perfect parent. No one is. We all have our faults and failures. Therefore, my children need to heal from the faults and failures of their dad, as I need to heal from the faults and failures of my parents. That's only natural. And to deny such a need is, again, to squander our power. Family-of-origin healing need not take forever, can even be fun with a competent therapist. Sort out all those old stories and discern in them the deeper truths. Find a healthy space to forgive and let go. We need not carry those burdens all our lives.

Spiritual Renewal: I want to dedicate a whole chapter to spiritual power, so let me just say here that to assume we are not spiritual creatures is to kick out one of the essential legs of our stress-management tripod. Try to make a tripod stand on just two legs. Won't work.

Power Over Stress – This means we take all this seriously. Enhance our chances by building a strong and durable stress management tripod – body, mind and spirit. To fail to do so is to give away an enormous amount of our power.

Building A Power Portfolio

- Which part of your stress management tripod; body, mind or spirit, needs the most attention at this time?
  - Where can you get that assistance?
  - Who will help you?
- In Nurture, what needs the most attention right now: learning, support, therapy, spiritual, leisure, friends or calling?
  - How can you get that help?
- In Advocacy, what needs the most attention right now: goals, calendar, job, boundaries, compensation?
  - How can you get the help you need?
- In Wholeness, what needs the most attention right now: exercise, nutrition, addiction, relaxation, meditation, marriage, family, or spirit?
  - How can you get the help you need?

NOTE: DO NOT ATTEMPT TO ADDRESS MORE THAN TWO OR THREE OF THESE ISSUES AT ONE TIME. YOU WILL ONLY OVERLOAD YOURSELF AND BE COUNTERPRODUCTIVE.

14. Investing in Your Spiritual Power

As I have mentioned, I am convinced that we are made up of three parts – body, mind (intellect and emotions) and spirit. This chapter is dedicated to a deeper understanding of the spiritual part of our lives and the power that can be gained by a healthy spiritual maturity.

There is ample research to assert that having a healthy spiritual life and being a part of a faith community can play a significant role in our wellbeing and even wellness.

Dr. Herbert Benson, a research physician at Harvard, wrote a best seller, *The Relaxation Response* (HarperCollins). In that, he demonstrated that people who practice relaxation and meditation are healthier. They can respond to a stressor and move into arousal quicker and more effectively. And when the stressor is removed or nullified, those who meditate regularly return more fully into homeostasis. That whole response mechanism functions better.

After that book, Benson wrote another – *Beyond the Relaxation Response: How to Harness the Healing Power of Your Personal Beliefs* (Time Books). In it, he shared the research evidence that people who have strong faith/belief systems and participate regularly in a faith community also have a stronger and more effective stress-response system. This empowers them to have a healthier and more rewarding life.

I want to emphasize this – a healthy and mature faith/belief system and conscientious participation in a faith community gives us another dimension of power and will otherwise increase our good health. This is more than knowing how to use the right power currencies or choosing the correct power conflict strategy. It is more than knowing when to use a polarity or the intricacies of our personality types, etc.

Spiritual power is birthed deeply within us and flows out in ways that comfort, empower and inspire us to courage and hope.

There has even been research to determine the existence of the soul. Dr. MacDougal measured the weight of a person the moment before they died and then again immediately after death. Dr. MacDougal recorded a difference of 21 grams (0.7408 ounces). There was no fluid lost or anything else removed from the body to account for this weight differential. It is therefore assumed that this loss of weight is attributed to the soul leaving the body.

While there is no tangible organ or part of the body that can be located and identified a "the soul," this weight loss cannot be accounted for any other way.

I suspect some will find this bizarre or unbelievable. That's okay; it is not essential to accept this assertion. I merely add it as further evidence of a spiritual part of our being.

And let me immediately state that while I have a faith system that works well for me, I am in no way declaring that there is only one correct faith/belief system and all others are wrong.

Let me assert that I find lots of enlightening aspects in a variety of faith/belief systems.

I have spent some time in South Korea, which is a predominately Buddhist country. I am impressed with the Buddhist passion for peace and harmony with all creation. People, plants, animals, water and air should be in one accord and live pleasantly with each other. I like that.

In Judaism, I find an orderliness that is impressive. Keeping a kosher lifestyle also binds people together and connects them to a rich heritage.

In Sikhism, I am impressed with the goal of connecting with God (or the Holy) in a selfless search for the truth.

In the Mormon (Latter-day Saints) faith, I love the emphasis on the family. At least one evening a week, the nuclear family is supposed to be together for dinner and loving conversation. No sports or other activities are allowed to compete with this important time for family bonding.

I am not a legitimate scholar of Islam, but I am confident that in the Qur'an there are passages I could affirm.

Lao Tzu is the founder of Taoism. Lao Tzu has many excellent sayings:

"If you don't change direction, you will end up where you are heading."

"Being deeply loved by someone gives you strength, while loving someone deeply gives you courage."

My favorite saying of Lao Tzu is "Where there is Light, call it Light." Which is to say, where there is truth, call it truth. Where there is love, call it love. Where there is wisdom, call it wisdom.

I want to affirm that many faith/belief systems have value. I do not want to be a religious bigot.

I know which faith/belief system works best for me. And I know how powerfully it enriches my life.

Simply as a means to illustrate the point, I want to share my faith system in Christianity. This is not to convert or challenge anyone. I want to present this as the kind of similar illustration I have done in other chapters.

When I insist that there is such a thing as spiritual power, what do I mean and how does it work for me? That's my purpose in sharing my faith. Not to proselytize.

For me the essential factor in being a Christian is obviously Jesus. History clearly documents that there was a person, Jesus, from Nazareth. He was an itinerate preacher who moved from town to town teaching and preaching a new way of living. Originally, this movement was called The Way.

Eventually, Jesus was crucified and buried. Now comes the tricky part. While crucified on a Friday, the following Sunday he was alive again.

Alive, not like someone who was resuscitated. To be resuscitated is to be alive only to die again sometime in the future. Jesus was not resuscitated. Jesus was resurrected – alive again on the other side of death. Alive again as one who is victorious over death. One who is never to die again because death is now in his past.

There are numerous eyewitnesses to this fact. In 1 Corinthians 15:6, we read, "Then he appeared to more than five hundred brothers and sisters at one time..." Either Jesus was really there, or we have an account of mass hallucination. I prefer to believe the historic record of all these eyewitnesses to the fact that once dead, this Jesus managed to defeat death and become alive again on the other side of death.

If the tomb is empty, that changes everything. And if the tomb is not empty, then I am wrong. I choose to accept the great tradition and belief that the tomb is empty. By the way, I have been to the Holy Land and have seen the empty tomb for myself. It is a pilgrimage I recommend.

So, given that this Jesus, from Nazareth, did in fact conquer death, what does that mean?

Next comes another "leap of faith." I also accept the teaching that this Jesus was no ordinary person. What made it possible for Jesus to defeat death is that Jesus is both human and divine. As the scriptures say, the Son of God and the Son of Man. Mary's boy and God's son.

This death of Jesus was for a purpose. God became human to take on our nature and even more. Jesus' mission was to assume the burden of all our "sins." Jesus was to be the sacrificial lamb to take away the sin of the entire world. A big leap of faith, to be sure. But let's go with it and see where it leads.

Therefore, Jesus' victory over death is also a victory over all the sins of the world. This grants all humans a grace undeserved and unearned. That is also an essential part of my faith system.

We call this story of Jesus the Gospel.

Gospel literally means "good news." It is emphatic good news that the tomb is empty and that all sins have been redeemed, forgiven.

My "good news" faith system cannot therefore assert that there is something I must do to earn my redemption or salvation. "If you don't accept Jesus as your Lord and Savior, you cannot go to Heaven." That's NOT good news. That's bad news. Because whatever you insist that I need to do to deserve my redemption or salvation will condemn me. Whatever it is, I am certain I will never do it *enough*. Enough is a key work in my spiritual vocabulary. I may try diligently, but I will never get it perfect, flawed mortal that I am. So, if it in any way to depends on my success at achieving whatever one insists I must do to merit my redemption that will only condemn me – and that is bad news.

The good news is that Jesus, once and for all, died and defeated death to earn for all people the hope and assurance of Heaven – period!

So, the Gospel gives me good news.

Further, the Gospel gives me hope. It is a hope unlike any other hope because it is a hope based on Jesus – who cannot die. So, the hope Jesus gives cannot fail. No other source of hope can make that claim. If we hope in our finances, education, physical prowess, good looks, whatever – all those are fragile and can fail. No temporal hope will endure. But the hope that Jesus provides is eternal and cannot be defeated – that battle is already won.

In addition, the Gospel gives me unconditional love. Jesus loves me *regardless*. There is nothing I can do to deserve Jesus' love. It is pure gift. It is grace.

Jesus does NOT say, "I will love you *if*..." Jesus states boldly, "I do love you *regardless*..."

So, Jesus' love is unconditional in that it is *without* condition.

Jesus' love is also unconditional in that it is *beyond* all human conditions.

To say, "I love you," is to make a promise. Every promise on the face of this earth has at least three conditions:

- Sincerity
- Capable
- Alive

To say, "I love you," is to beg the question, do I really mean it? We hope so.

But when Jesus says, "I love you," Jesus backed that up with his death on the Cross and his victory over the tomb. That's solid evidence of sincerity. We can trust Jesus. He has earned that big time.

Is Jesus capable of loving every human being – every man, woman and child now alive, or who was alive, or whoever will be alive? YES, because Jesus is God. And God is infinite. So, Jesus' love is infinite, without dimensions, endless.

Finally, will death stop Jesus from loving us all? NO. Jesus has defeated death. Death cannot stop Jesus from loving. Where else can we get such confidence?

Jesus' love for us is unconditional – without any conditions – and beyond all conditions.

Finally, Jesus gives us an open future. Because of the forgiveness and confidence found through Jesus, our future is no longer determined by our past. We are free to be all God wants us to be. Nothing holds us back except our own faults and failures, our weaknesses and selfishness.

An open future is ours to claim if we dare.

That good news, hope, unconditional love and open future empowers me to dare to venture into each new day with a strength and courage I cannot find elsewhere.

Let me give another kind of illustration. A rising phenomenon in our culture is the response "none," when asked "What is your religious preference?" More and more people have no religious or faith/belief system active in their lives.

In order to better understand this, I did a little case study. I interviewed a number of students from Anne Arundel Community College with the assistance of Dr. Gina Finelli of the sociology department. These students all identified their religious preference as none.

I stated that I had no intention of converting them or changing their minds, I just wanted to understand.

I asked them four questions.

The first question was to explain what having "none" as their religious preference meant to them. After some conversation, I reflected that it sounded like they were "indifferent" toward the church – they neither had a negative or a positive impression. They were second or third generation "unchurched." Church played no relevant role in their lives. They were indifferent.

Second, I asked them to tell me about hope. Third, I asked them to tell me about trust. In both cases, they initially stumbled and paused. Finally, they defined both hope and trust in transactional terms. If I am trustworthy and you are trustworthy, then trust can exist between us. If I am a person in whom one can confidently have hope and you are the same, then hope can exist between us. Transactional. There was no deep or universal well of hope and trust of which they were aware, nor could they access. Both were purely transactional.

Finally, I asked them what happens when they die. None seemed to be at all anxious about that. Most had no idea, but it was not threatening. A few had some belief in a positive afterlife but had no idea why or where. Interestingly, none believed in Hell.

Second- and third-generation young adults unchurched – and they had no sense at all that there could be some universal and dependable source of hope and trust to sustain their lives and give them a confidence to embrace whatever came their way. They said things like:

- Trust is conditional.
- Trust only can exist between friends and family.
- It is not good to just trust; we need to be cautious.

The comments were similar regarding hope. For these students, trust and hope were not anchored in anything found deeply within their souls. It was merely based on transactional, and therefore fragile, dependence.

Those comments make perfect sense if one's hope and trust abide in sources that are merely temporal or transactional. But if one has a source of hope and trust that is abiding, durable and exists deeply within one's soul, that is entirely different.

I do affirm that there is a universal source of enduring hope and trust – of love and acceptance – that I can claim for my life that not only empowers me for all the challenges of each new day but also takes away from me the fear of death and the anxiety of tomorrow.

I have Good News, Hope and Unconditional Love, and my future is wide open for me to be all that God wants me to be. That is powerful. That is what I mean by spiritual power.

It is a faith system that is reinforced by participation in a faith fellowship of like believers. Without that, I, too, would be reduced to merely transactional efforts that are based on temporal conditions that are not definitely dependable.

There is such a thing as spiritual power.

Find the faith/belief system that works for you as Christianity works for me. Engage in that system and associate with fellow believers. It is empowering.

Building A Power Portfolio

- What do you base hope and trust on in your life?
  - How is that working for you?
  - How deep is that understanding?
- Is there a faith/belief system that benefits you?
  - How do you define that?
- What could make your faith/belief system more effective?
- To what extent does your faith/belief system empower your life?
  - How could that be better?

15. Creating a Well-Balanced Power Portfolio

In this chapter, I thought it would be fun to share a number of my personal axioms by which I live – or attempt to live.

Most of these are lighthearted but do reflect some deeper significance. Enjoy them and choose which ones you might want to adopt.

Don't agonize, organize

While the meaning of this is rather obvious, I confess that I have very little patience for folks who love to wallow in their agony. Okay, things are tough. I get it. Now, what are you going to do about it?

Remember the short-term solutions therapy? The truth is that people have more coping skills than they give themselves credit for. Asking, "How have you managed so far?" helps to bring to the surface some recognition of those coping and problem-solving skills. Now that they are in one's awareness, let's put them to use.

To organize often means to assess one's resources. "Do I have what I need to deal with this issue on my own?" "If not, what am I missing?" "Where can I get it?" "When can I get started?" And here's a good one – "Who will keep me accountable for following through?" That's the kind of thing I mean by organizing.

Map out a plan. Don't just agonize. Take charge. Be a victor, not a victim!

To capitulate is to perpetuate

To get a bit spiritual – there are two kinds of sins: commission and omission. To commit a sin is to do something wrong. But a sin of omission is to fail to do what is right and needed.

To capitulate when action is needed is to condone the wrong and allow it to continue. Complaining is not a solution. When there is wrongdoing or injustice, it needs to be labeled and exposed – even if that means an internal soul searching. To claim our own faults and failures is a wonderful first step, but to leave it at that is to capitulate to the error. To rise above our shortcomings requires that we own them, claim them and then address them in a solution that may require numerous steps.

When working with others in any capacity, the strength to speak out and name a problem is a much-needed behavior for that group or organization to be healthy. Too many members fail to speak out against problems or injustice.

There's a famous quote from Pastor Niemoller during Nazi Germany. "First, they came for the Socialists, and I did not speak out – because I was not a Socialist. Then they came for the Trade Unionists, and I did not speak out – because I was not a Trade Unionist. Then they came for the Jews, and I did not speak out – because I was not a Jew. Then they came for me – and there was no one left to speak out for me."

To say nothing is to condone. And that can make matters terribly worse.

Claim your voice. Speak out. Do not submit. Stand firm. Fight for the right. Be brave and strong. Gandhi said, "One with the truth is a majority."

Don't oppose unless you propose

I'm also very tired of people who just complain and don't do anything to solve the problem. Speaking out is good and right. But don't leave it at that.

Perhaps even before speaking out, do some homework and seek some possible solutions. Notice I said solution**s** – plural. No one expects each of us to always be right. So, don't wait until we have the problem resolved before we say something.

Further, to look only at binary solutions – this or that – often does not lead to the best resolution. By simply adding more options, it gets us out of binary thinking and into a more creative kind of processing. Even if the third option is nonsense, it moves our problem-solving methods from binary to creative. And even if we choose one of the original binary options, just the fact that we came to that conclusion in a more creative process will lend the answer a greater chance for success.

So, don't oppose unless you propose a variety of options – some may even be purely crazy, but they open up the problem-solving process to a more creative methodology.

If you always do what you always did, you'll always get what you always got

Apparently, many have laid claim to this saying, from Albert Einstein to Henry Ford to Mark Twain. I make no claim that this is my own, but I still like it.

Another way this is sometimes said is, "Insanity is doing the same thing over and over and expecting different results."

Always doing the same thing and then hoping there will be a different outcome makes no sense. If we want or need a different outcome, we will need to exhibit different behaviors or harbor different attitudes.

Repeating a problematic behavior only exacerbates the problem. Remember the polarity graph? When something works, simply doing more and more of it often drives the results into the negative quadrant. To get positive results, one needs to move to the other side of the graph – the opposite quadrant. Then we need to monitor that behavior so that it doesn't fall into the negative quadrant.

Repetition is rarely a solution. Sounds more like a bad habit.

You are as sick as your secrets

The more secrets I hold deeply in my heart and mind, the more they will fester and be toxic. To be cured of those negative secrets, I need to own them in a therapeutic way and exorcise them. Often, this needs professional help.

Similarly, the more secrets a family hides, the more pathological the family environment is for everyone in it. To have a healthy family system is to follow the systems theory of surrounding the pathogen with "antidotes" and negate and expel the pathogen. The best antidote is often the truth. "Yes, Dad has a drinking problem and we are no longer going to tolerate it. We're going to help Dad."

Likewise, in any organization the more secrets (not counting trade secrets) in an organization – yes, the boss does that bad behavior, but let's just not talk about it, we don't want to cause trouble – only make matters worse. And the boss should be the one most invested in the health of the organization!

Secrets are most often pathogens in a system of any kind. They poison the system and keep it from being healthy and reaching its desired goals. Hoarding those secrets will only make things worse. Address them properly and surround them with healthy behaviors that will negate and hopefully eliminate them from the system.

Beware of the bland leading the bland

That is not a typo. It is a take on the blind leading the blind. The two key words in this axiom are "bland" and "leading."

By bland, I mean those who are non-productive and simply exist in a system but make no great contribution. They may show up day after day and perform their dutiful tasks somewhat grudgingly and without passion or delight. They may cause no problems, but they also seldom offer any creative or inspiring ideas. They are just there – bland.

"Leading" implies that there is some leadership responsibility involved. Actually, in a healthy system, every person has leadership responsibilities. When all the leadership rests on only one shoulder, that's hoarding the power and thus diminishing the power and creativity and inspiration of all the other participants. When everyone in the system is respected and expected to make leadership suggestions and infuse the system with spirit and inspiration, the system is far more healthy and powerful.

The bland leading the bland happens too often. As a result, the system slowly deteriorates and fails to reach its goals. A key symptom of this is when a system refuses to address the changes in the culture and tries to remain the same forever. Those who made wagon wheels went out of business because they identified themselves as in the wagon wheel business. If they had identified themselves as in the transportation business and evolved with the times, they would still be in business in a new way.

It's impossible to have a "wrong" feeling

It's not our feelings that get us into trouble or rob us of our power. It's what we do with our feelings.

Okay, you treated me with disrespect. Now I'm angry. I probably have every right to be angry. I was disrespected. BUT what am I going to do with that anger? Will I punch you in the face? That will probably only make matters worse. Will I subjugate the anger and let it fester within me? That won't help either. What if I calmly replied, "Wow, that was hurtful. I suspect you really didn't mean to be hurtful. Let's talk about this." I have turned my anger into a more positive way to resolve the situation.

Feelings are just that – feelings. None of them are wrong. They just are.

Let me repeat that. No feeling is a wrong feeling. What is wrong and internally hurtful is to deny the feeling or subjugate the feeling or let the feeling run amok. We really don't have to **do** anything with a feeling other than acknowledge it and claim it. "Oh, I'm angry. That's interesting. What do I want to do with that? What behavior will be a positive and helpful response?"

It's our behaviors that get us into trouble – not our feelings.

Own the feelings. Claim them. Explore them. EIAG them. Then move forward in a helpful way and express yourself appropriately.

Know the difference between humility and humiliation

I'm all in favor of appropriate humility. Being properly humble is a good thing.

One can be too humble and cross into putting oneself down and degrading oneself. I'm all against that. Does no one any good.

But a healthy dose of humility can be beneficial.

However, humiliation is something entirely different.

Humiliation moves into the degrading range. It attempts to rob one of their dignity and self-worth.

Remember Viktor Frankl in the concentration camp. While the whole system was organized to degrade, Frankl recognized that people can only take our dignity and our self-worth away from us if we let them.

I am totally against humiliation in any form. It turns people into objects and that is wrong. Do not tolerate it. Organize. Hold fast to your dignity. Stand tall. And be powerful!

Things can be so heavenly minded they are no earthly good

For someone who so strongly advocates for the spiritual aspect as part of personal power, this may be surprising. But we do not live in Heaven. We live in a mortal existence.

To impose upon us "heavenly solutions" is just not going to work. This is one reason I encourage all of us to take ourselves seriously – limits and all.

At age 70+ and only five feet six inches tall, it is highly unlikely that I will be able to dunk a basketball. No use even trying.

So, to lay on me the expectation of dunking a basketball, no matter how noble the reason or cause, would result in failure.

We can hold up the heavenly as an aspirational ideal. We can dedicate ourselves to strive faithfully in those directions. But to expect heavenly results is to only set us up for failure. I'm all against setting people up for failure. It wastes power.

Aspire for the heavenly, and then strive for the real progress in a heavenly direction.

I have the right to be wrong

I am merely mortal. I am not a god – never have been, never will be.

So, embracing my mortality I affirm that from time to time, I will make mistakes. I have faults and failures. I do things I wish I didn't do, and I fail to do things I wish I had done.

To torture myself for my imperfections is nonsense. You shouldn't do it either.

I affirm that I screw up from time to time. Own it, address it properly and move on.

Yes, mere mortal that I am, I will be wrong now and then. I have that right. So, do you.

A simple answer to a complex problem is usually wrong

I am frustrated by people who face a complex problem – like most problems really are – and someone provides a simplistic solution and expects everyone to be in awe. Really?

No. We are complex creatures. Simply solutions rarely work.

Remember the mobile in the systems theory discussion? Make one change here and the whole mobile needs to rebalance itself. That leads to more and more issues in an ongoing way.

Humans and our organizations (especially families) are far too complex for simple solutions. We need to appreciate that fact.

Okay, we make this change here. What can we anticipate as a result? How will things be out of balance? What next step can we predict? How can we prepare for that before we make the first change? What needs to be in place? Let's address this in a holistic manner.

Simple answers may work for little children. They are more concrete in their thinking and want things on their level. For them, that's fine.

But we adults need to be much more mature and sophisticated. Simplicity won't work for us and for our systems. So, take on the problems but do so in a more advanced and holistic fashion.

The power of forgiveness

This is a spinoff from "don't agonize, organize."

Okay, something was done against us. We have been transgressed. That's a fact. Now we have a choice. Will we harbor that hurt or will we do something about it?

As I have said, letting hurt infest us with endless discomfort and pain gets us nowhere. Honor the feeling. We have been hurt and the pain is real. Embrace it.

But to hold onto it and endure it gets us nowhere.

Now, I need to firmly state that forgiveness and justice are two different things. Just because I forgive does not mean that justice is inappropriate. Someone did something wrong. I can forgive them, but they still need to face the justice for their transgression. Those two do not oppose each other.

My desire to forgive can guide me to better understand why they did what they did. What mitigated that action? Is there some underlying cause that needs to be addressed, and can we be agents to help resolve those conditions? Why did this happen? What can I do about it?

To get stuck in our pain and refuse to forgive impedes my efforts to see that this never happens again to anyone.

The power of forgiveness empowers me to get beyond the pain, understand the complexity of the situation and be a productive force for change.

Further, forgiveness lifts a burden from our souls we do not need to endure. That, in itself, is empowering.

Well, there you have them. A range of the personal power axioms I try to live by. It is plain to see where power can be derived or deprived. Adopt any or all as you may.

Building A Power Portfolio

- Which of these axioms resonates most with you? Why?
- What can you do to adapt the wisdom of any of these axioms?
    - Who can help you do that?
- Which of these axioms speaks to your family context? Why?
    - What can you do about that?
- Which of these axioms applies to your work/school environment? Why?
    - What can you do about that?

Final Personal Power Portfolio Checkup

You took this checkup at the beginning of the book. Now that you have followed each chapter and applied the concepts in your own life, retake this checkup and compare your responses. For each item, note the response that most accurately defines your actions most of the time.

1. Have you lost sleep because of the behavior (i.e. comments, etc.) of someone else?

    Never   Seldom   Sometimes   Often

2. Have you extracted one or more promises from a friend or family member regarding *their behavior* toward you or others which that person did not keep?

    Never   Seldom   Sometimes   Often

3. Do many or most of your thoughts revolve around issues with your family/friends/colleagues around their behaviors?

    Never   Seldom   Sometimes   Often

4. Do you make decisions and do not follow through with them; especially if you are worried about how that decision might impact another?

    Never   Seldom   Sometimes   Often

5. Has your attitude changed/fluctuated toward one or more members of your family, friends, colleagues? (For example:

alternating between love and anger or contempt or indifference)

Never   Seldom   Sometimes   Often

6. Do you think everything would be okay if only a troublesome member of your family, a friend, a colleague would stop or control his/her troublesome behavior?

Never   Seldom   Sometimes   Often

7. Have your moods changed drastically as a result of a member of your family, a friend, a colleague's mood or behavior?

Never   Seldom   Sometimes   Often

8. Do you feel guilty and/or responsible for the mood or behavior of a family member, friend, or colleague?

Never   Seldom   Sometimes   Often

9. Do you try to conceal or deny problems, make excuses, or protect a member of your family, a friend, a colleague?

Never   Seldom   Sometimes   Often

10. Have you withdrawn from outside activities and/or social contacts because of worry over the behavior of a family member, a friend, a colleague?

Never   Seldom   Sometimes   Often

11. Have you withdrawn from outside activities and/or friends because you were too busy or too tired?

Never   Seldom   Sometimes   Often

12. Have you taken over responsibilities or duties that were formerly done by a member of your family, a friend, a colleague should have done?

   Never   Seldom   Sometimes   Often

13. Do you feel hopeless and defeated, that nothing you can do will improve the situation?

   Never   Seldom   Sometimes   Often

14. Do you feel you give more than you receive in relationships?

   Never   Seldom   Sometimes   Often

15. Is it difficult for you to feel good about yourself when others are angry or critical of you?

   Never   Seldom   Sometimes   Often

16. Do you have difficulty expressing your feelings, especially anger, because of fear about how others will react?

   Never   Seldom   Sometimes   Often

17. Do you say "yes" when you would like to say "no," do things for others that you resent, or feel guilty when you say "no" to others?

   Never   Seldom   Sometimes   Often

18. Do you try to appear cheerful when you're hurting inside?

   Never   Seldom   Sometimes   Often

19. Have you violated the privacy of others in order to check up on

them? (For example: reading their mail, checking their e-mail or voice mail, etc.)

Never   Seldom   Sometimes   Often

20. Have you violated your own values in order to avoid conflict or feel accepted or connected with others?

Never   Seldom   Sometimes   Often

21. Have you done many things for others that they could do for themselves because you enjoy feeling needed?

Never   Seldom   Sometimes   Often

22. Have you done many things for others that they could do for themselves because you think you can do it better than they would, or you don't want to inconvenience them?

Never   Seldom   Sometimes   Often

23. Do you not tell others about your problems because you don't trust they will really care or understand, and you don't like to bother them?

Never   Seldom   Sometimes   Often

24. Do you pride yourself in your ability to go without and to endure pain and hardship?

Never   Seldom   Sometimes   Often

25. Have you neglected your own responsibilities and your performance has suffered because of your worry about others?

Never   Seldom   Sometimes   Often

26. Have you been engaging in some behaviors (for example: eating, working, drinking, sex, gambling, spending, etc.) more than you feel comfortable with?

Never   Seldom   Sometimes   Often

27. Do you feel somewhat righteous or superior to others?

Never   Seldom   Sometimes   Often

28. Are you unhappy when a member of your family, a friend, a colleague is unhappy or is behaving inappropriately?

Never   Seldom   Sometimes   Often

29. Has your relationship with another been affected by feelings of anger, fear, contempt, disappointment, or distrust?

Never   Seldom   Sometimes   Often

30. Do you think that if the troublesome other really liked you they would stop their problematic behavior?

Never   Seldom   Sometimes   Often

31. Do you feel if you could just try harder to be more pleasant, patient, fun, interesting, exciting, or kind the troublesome other would stop their problematic behavior?

Never   Seldom   Sometimes   Often

32. Are you afraid that other people blame you for the troublesome behavior of another?

Never   Seldom   Sometimes   Often

33. Have you been physically or verbally abusive to a troublesome other when angry or upset about that person's behavior?

Never   Seldom   Sometimes   Often

34. Do you feel more like a parent to a friend or colleague?

Never   Seldom   Sometimes   Often

35. Do you feel forced to exert tight control over another with less and less success while financial problems increase?

Never   Seldom   Sometimes   Often

36. Have you been angry or impatient and lashed out at another because you were really worried or angry at someone else?

Never   Seldom   Sometimes   Often

37. Do you feel shame for staying in a relationship and putting up with troublesome behavior with another for so long but are afraid to drop the relationship?

Never   Seldom   Sometimes   Often

38. Do others accuse you of taking things too seriously?

Never   Seldom   Sometimes   Often

39. Do others accuse you of being too impatient, critical or demanding?

Never   Seldom   Sometimes   Often

40. Do you make extra efforts to please others because it is very important that they accept you personally and won't reject

you?

Never   Seldom   Sometimes   Often

Looking at your responses, any "Often" responses are an issue and worth investigating – perhaps with a therapist. If you have a pattern of frequent "Often" responses – then therapy is definitely in order. The more your responses lean in that direction, the more attention is worthy.

On the other hand, if your pattern is "Never" or leaning toward "Never," all is well and good. Congratulations – IF YOU HAVE BEEN HONEST WITH YOURSELF.

If your responses have not changed from the initial checkup, you may not have applied the concepts as intended. Everyone learns at their own pace, so try going back through the book until these concepts become second nature.

Your power. Stop giving it away.

Bibliography

Benson, Herbert (1975). *The Relaxation Response*, Harper Collins; (1984) *Beyond the Relaxation Response: How to Harness the Healing Power of Your Personal Beliefs*. Time Books.

Bolsinger, Tod (2015). *Canoeing the Mountains*. IVP.

Farquhar, John (1978). *The American Way of Life Need Not Be Hazardous to Your Health*. W.H. Norton & Co.

Harris, Thomas (1969). *I'm Okay, You're Okay*. Harper Collins.

Heath, Chip & Don (2010). *Switch: How to Change Things When Change is Hard*. Broadway Books.

Johnson, Barry (1992). *Polarity Management: Identifying and Managing Unsolvable Problems*. HDR Press.

Lehr, Fred (1982). *Helping People Understand and Manage Your Stress*. Drew University.

MacDougall, Duncan (1907). *21 Grams Experiment*. Haverhill, MA.

Myers, IB, et al, (1998). *MBTI Manual: A Guide to the Development and Use of the Myers-Briggs Type Indicator*. Palo, Alto: Consulting Psychologists Press.

Parsons, George (1989). *Intervening in a Church Fight: A Manual for Internal Consultants*. Alban Institute.

Pelletier, Kenneth (1997). *Mind as Healer, Mind as Slayer*. Delacorte Press/S. Lawrence.

Selye, Hans (1956). *The Stress of Life*. McGregor Hill.

Also note: Mid-Atlantic Association for Training And Consulting, no longer in existence.

About the Author

Dr. Fred Lehr has a BA in Sociology from Susquehanna University, a Master of Divinity from Lutheran Theological Seminary, and a Doctor of Ministry from Drew University. He has spent his professional career focusing on family dynamics, stress management, spiritual wellness, and behavioral science. Dr. Lehr is certified by the National Council on Family Relations as a Family Life Educator (Emeritus), certified Myers-Briggs Type Indicator (MBTI) and Life Orientations (LIFO) trainer. Listed in 4th edition of *Who's Who in Religion*. He is the author of several books including:

- *Becoming a 21st Century Church: A Transformational Manual*, Wipf and Stock, 2017
- *Clergy Burnout: Recovering from the 70 Hour Work Week and Other Self-Defeating Practices*, Augsburg Press, 2006
- *After-words in the Upper Room*, a chancel drama, 1996
- *Helping People Understand and Manage Their Stress: A Pastoral/Educational Approach*, Drew University, 1982

CPSIA information can be obtained
at www.ICGtesting.com
Printed in the USA
FSHW020212211120
75950FS